'Most children are able to interpret and respond to social contexts and cues in school with incredible speed and without effort. For others, like those diagnosed with autism, the events and interactions of each day hold elusive meanings and unforeseen pitfalls. Growing to middle childhood and beyond, the challenges compound exponentially. School poses an increasing threat full of new (and abstract!) words and concepts (such as practice and revision), incomprehensible events (such as raffles), and unspoken rules of all kinds. These children crave a comprehensible clarification of numerous contexts in school that are so obvious to their peers. Social Stories™ are like a magic wand that replaces confusion with information and fear with confidence, to build social competence one Story at a time. Siobhan Timmins shares the Social Stories and Social Articles that have helped her son to find to find his way, in his own way. Siobhan does not only know how to write Social Stories that are very empowering, she elevates them to a parenting style. Every child with autism dreams of a mother like Siobhan, a mother who clarifies the world in such a way that her child not only becomes less confused and worried, but can flourish and thrive.'

— *Peter Vermeulen, PhD, Senior Lecturer at Autisme Centraal, Belgium. Author of over 15 books on autism including* Autism as Context Blindness, *2012*

'She has done it again! Dr Siobhan Timmins previously gave us the best possible guidance for using social stories for young children, and this new book addresses secondary school and college students. The context-setting that helps further understanding of autistic thinking is superb, as are the examples of the social stories themselves. My personal favourite is "Why do senior school teachers use loud voices?" If this were a "must-have" for every school and college, life for autistic children would be that much better.'

— *Jude Ragan, ex-head of Queensmill School, freelance autism education specialist*

'As a professional who works with young adults with autism in a day setting, I found this book very useful. In particular the sections about how sometimes the individual may not understand that they have to wait for help when you are helping others and how to address this in a suitable way.

It was great to see examples of the social stories and even better to read about real life experiences the author has had with her son. I would definitely recommend this book to anyone that either knows someone with autism personally or works in this type of setting, particularly the school setting.'

– Lisa Faulkner

Successful Social Stories™ for School and College Students with Autism

by the same author

Successful Social Stories™ for Young Children with Autism
Growing Up with Social Stories™
Dr Siobhan Timmins
Foreword by Carol Gray
ISBN 978 1 78592 112 4
eISBN 978 1 78450 376 5

Successful Social Stories™ for Young Adults with Autism
Growing Up with Social Stories™
Dr Siobhan Timmins
Foreword by Carol Gray
ISBN 978 1 78592 138 4
eISBN 978 1 78450 403 8

Developing Resilience in Young People with
Autism using Social Stories™
Dr Siobhan Timmins
ISBN 978 1 78592 329 6
eISBN 978 1 78450 643 8

of related interest

My Social Stories™ Book
Edited by Carol Gray and Abbie Leigh White
Illustrated by Sean McAndrew
ISBN 978 1 85302 950 9
eISBN 978 0 85700 166 5

SUCCESSFUL SOCIAL STORIES™
FOR SCHOOL AND COLLEGE STUDENTS WITH AUTISM

GROWING UP WITH SOCIAL STORIES™

DR SIOBHAN TIMMINS

FOREWORD BY CAROL GRAY

Jessica Kingsley *Publishers*
London and Philadelphia

First published in 2017
by Jessica Kingsley Publishers
73 Collier Street
London N1 9BE, UK
and
400 Market Street, Suite 400
Philadelphia, PA 19106, USA

www.jkp.com

Library of Congress Cataloging in Publication Data
A CIP catalog record for this book is available from the Library of Congress

British Library Cataloguing in Publication Data
A CIP catalogue record for this book is available from the British Library

ISBN 978 1 78592 137 7
eISBN 978 1 78450 404 5

Printed and bound in Great Britain

This book is dedicated to my son Mark,
who faces all challenges with
an honesty, courage and dignity
that humbles me daily.

He continues to be my inspiration.

Contents

Noise in School

Foreword
Carol Gray

It is a rare honor to write this foreword for *Successful Social Stories for School and College Students*. I wrote the foreword for the first book in the *Growing Up with Social Stories* series. I will also be writing the foreword for the third and final volume. A 'continuing foreword' fits the unprecedented uniqueness of this collection of Social Stories and Social Articles developed by Dr. Siobhan Timmins, for her son, Mark. I feel privileged as the 'moderator' of their story about growing up with Social Stories.

Early in 1994, Siobhan's son, Mark, was diagnosed with autism. She left her practice to search for answers and discovered Social Stories at one of my workshops. Siobhan became her son's personal author. *Successful Social Stories for Young Children* is a collection of Mark's earliest Stories. In this book, Mark is older. Time has shifted the settings, people, triumphs and challenges in his life. Mark and Mum are in different locations for much of each day, and new people are involved with varying understandings of autism. To quote an often-used phrase, 'It's a whole new ball game' and Mark is always on the field. There is so much we can control when children are very young. Little by little, Mark is moving from Siobhan's reach. More of each day is up to Mark.

As children grow, they go – experiencing a world of new adults and peers without mum or dad at their side. It would seem that as parents we would welcome the 'break' that school provides.

For years we have looked forward to this day when our children are older and more independent. Now we're here, we've arrived; only to learn that yesterday was easier. Where previously we were awakened in the middle of the night by a toddler's cries – now we're the only ones awake. Parenting becomes increasingly difficult as new experiences and the number of people in a child's life increases. It is no wonder that so many early childhood education programs hold graduation ceremonies. Similar to completion of all formal education, what lies beyond early childhood is equally new and challenging for every child.

Adding autism to the 'growing up' equation intensifies the experience for parents, their children, and professionals working on their behalf. For Siobhan, autism puts a highlighter on everything in Mark's life. Everything. Take handwriting for example. Learning to write isn't easy. For a child with autism, 'everything' includes the challenge of forming letters and understanding important related concepts – like why written letters are going to vary a bit from those generated by a computer or printing press. What about words and their meanings? When playing a game, the word 'home' frequently refers to a goal or place on the playing field or game. Teaching everything includes learning the rules and new meanings for established vocabulary. Everything means that nothing is taken for granted when raising a child with autism. It's overwhelming.

For caregivers working on behalf of people with autism, there are many moments when overwhelmed knocks on the door. Overwhelmed is a potentially paralyzing feeling that arrives on the heels of a challenging situation or concern. Always unwelcome and uninvited, back once again. It's the feeling we try to push aside so that we can determine our next move, find a good solution. Overwhelmed blurs vision and consumes intelligent thought. We can't think as well as we usually do. In sharp contrast, it is here where Social Stories are most at ease; patient, comfortable, and powerful antidotes to feeling overwhelmed and not knowing what to do.

What Einstein was to atomic theory, astronomy, and math, Siobhan Timmins is to Social Stories™. Throughout this book, Siobhan aptly demonstrates how Social Stories help us to find the 'social simplicity' in those situations or circumstances that initially seem 'too big' or multi-faceted. She's a genius at it. Siobhan is a perfect teacher of how to respond to the many unforeseen elements of growing up with autism. She has the pre-requisite unassuming attitude, the patient gathering of information, the unfaltering quest for understanding, and the ability to use text and illustration to meaningfully and respectfully share information.

The only drawback I see to this series is that Siobhan makes the Social Story process and format look so very easy. Keep in mind that Social Stories require us to step aside from all of the factors, feelings, and interpretations that we have made all of our lives. Easy? Not for us; not for Siobhan, not for me, not for anyone. It's human nature: overwhelmed prefers to entertain equally complex and contrived solutions that complement its self-perceived depth of hopelessness. Most of us are so inherently socially and emotionally intricate that the simplicity of Social Stories may be 'hard to trust' as a viable solution to a challenging, lie-awake-at-night sort of situation.

The discrepancy between how we consider all that surrounds us – and Social Stories that introduce us to what we can't see as a result – may be genuinely frustrating; especially at first. To write a Social Story is the most humbling exercise we can engage in; for all the assumptions that it forces us to push aside, we are required to invest in a process that structures how to think over *our usual way of thinking*.

With this foreword, I ask you to step back and look at what you are holding. Regard the bigger picture. Mark is moving from early childhood to grade school and beyond. You'll feel overwhelmed along with Siobhan. Watch how she continues to patiently answer the door and how she develops Stories about topics that often baffle the masses. To date, I know of only one person, Dr. Siobhan Timmins, who is as steadfast in her trust in Social Stories™, as they are in their calm resolve to help each of us grow, one Story at a time.

Knock knock.

Carol Gray, Social Stories™ Founder and Author The New Social Story™ Book: Revised and Expanded 15th Anniversary Edition *www.CarolGraySocialStories.com*

Acknowledgements

Thanks first and foremost go to Mark, who has given his full permission for his Stories to be published so that other children may benefit from them.

I will always be profoundly grateful to Carol Gray for sharing her phenomenal insight into social understanding in autism, and introducing me to her Social Stories™ approach. Carol encouraged me to publish my Stories and has supported me throughout the process. I am so very grateful to her for sharing her friendship, wisdom and immense experience in this field.

Thanks too to Eileen Arnold, my Satellite mentor, for her continual guidance and support since I started as a coach in 2012.

Special thanks must go to Helen Barker, Mark's learning support assistant, who was absolutely critical to his success all through his school years. Stories would be written and read at home, and Helen was the person who read them with him in school. She will always be a very important person in both Mark's and our family life.

I would like to also thank Andrew Moore, the headmaster of Mark's school at the time, who had the compassion, vision and initiative to invite Mark to join his brothers there; thanks also to Gary Smith, headmaster of Market Field School, who supported and facilitated the transition.

Throughout his time at school and college Mark was taught and helped by so many people. There are far too many of you to name individually here, but you all know who you are, and I am sure you will remember Mark and the important individual contribution each one of you has made to his progress. We will always be grateful to you all!

I would also like to thank Jessica Kingsley and her team who have been so enthusiastic about bringing my Social Stories™ to people's bookshelves.

Lastly and most importantly I would like to thank my wonderful family for all their loving support without which I absolutely could never have written this book.

This book is a collection of successful Social Stories written for Mark, and others, as part of the 'Growing Up with Social Stories' series. This set of books aims to clearly demonstrate, with real-life examples, the phenomenal impact that the Social Stories approach can have across the lifespan of a young person with autism. This second book focuses on the school and college years.

Note on language

Throughout this book I have referred to the child as male, primarily because the Stories were mostly written originally for my son. However, they have been individualised and shared with success with other children, both male and female. So wherever the pronoun 'he' is used it is synonymous with 'she'.

I have also used the phrase 'child with autism' in preference to 'autistic child' as this is my son's personal choice. The word 'autism' used throughout is a synonym for 'autism spectrum condition'.

Understanding my child's perspective in school

Children with autism often display responses in school that are unexpected or unusual to teaching staff and classmates who do not have autism. Professionals frequently try to change these responses without success. This may lead to the assumption that the child knows what to do and is choosing not to do it. The child may even be labelled non-compliant or defiant. Developing a better understanding of how our children perceive the world explains these unusual responses. Improving insight into how our children think allows us to understand that the 'challenging' responses we are witnessing are in fact coping strategies, and 'inappropriate' responses are frequently completely appropriate for their understanding of an event or situation.

Young and old people with autism have a different social understanding of the world from neurotypical people. Within the school setting many of the aspects of the social world they find difficult are concentrated into a small space without the capacity to escape. Looking more closely at the specific situations that occur in school and unravelling them from the perspective of a person with autism helps us understand how we can help.

Understanding context

When neurotypical children and adults encounter a new situation we immediately get a sense of the essence of the situation. This essence or gist is known as the context of the situation. Recognition of the context happens without us having to think, in less than half the time it takes to blink an eye. Identifying the context allows our brain to focus on the cues in that situation that are socially relevant (Vermeulen, 2012). We can then make social sense of these cues, meanwhile ignoring all the other pieces of information that are streaming in through our senses. This allows our brain to take advantage of previous experience in a similar situation so we can predict what might happen next and recall safe and effective language and behaviour to use in the situation. This ability to notice the socially relevant cues and make social sense of them is called central coherence and happens for neurotypicals innately, is never taught or learned and cannot be switched off.

Children with autism encountering a new situation are less able to identify and *use* the context to focus on the socially relevant cues and so focus instead on the ones that interest them (Vermeulen, 2012). This 'Context Blindness' as described by Vermeulen means they lack information from the socially relevant cues and therefore may not make social sense of the situation. This is described as having weak central coherence and results in the child having less ability to predict what is coming next and to choose safe and effective social responses for that situation. The situation might be an interaction with another person like a classmate or teacher, or an environment like a lesson or an assembly. The child may therefore respond in a way that does not match the expected behaviour for that situation and may be mistakenly described as 'inappropriate'. In fact, the response may be completely appropriate for their perception of the situation.

In a similar way children with autism often have difficulty making social sense of the cues involved in facial expressions, tone of voice and body language in other people. They may be less able to discern how these cues give a collective sense of the emotion that person may be currently experiencing.

Understanding the context in school

In school there are numerous changing contexts happening throughout the day, many more than might occur at home. Children move from lesson to lesson, to the playground, dinner hall, gymnasium and assembly. They are asked to interact with the child sitting beside them, their learning support assistant (LSA), the teacher, the dinner lady, the playground supervisor, the headmaster. For each of these people there is an individual social context with an expected behaviour led by the context. The child with autism frequently misreads this and makes social mistake after social mistake.

As a consequence of this difficulty with context and making sense of a social situation, our children may be less able, or unable, to recognise when a situation is coming to an end and a new situation is beginning. Because any new situation is also difficult to quickly make sense of, change becomes frightening and disturbing and results in huge anxiety. In order to prevent change and to relieve this anxiety, our children may strive to control the people and objects in the environment and keep everything the same. They may feel reassured by structure and ritual, being soothed by repetitive activities. This may explain why they often enjoy watching the same YouTube clip or DVD over and over – perhaps the only time they can truly predict what is coming next.

In between lessons, the school puts in place activities to relax the children, such as break time, lunch time and sports as well as fun activities like school trips, sports day and charity days, all of which, instead of relaxing the child with autism, may ramp up their anxiety.

When comfortable in a familiar context the child with autism may manage quite well, but when a small change happens, like a different child sitting next to them, a substitute teacher or an expected task being cancelled, they are quickly bewildered and anxious.

Social Stories™ are stories that are written in a specific way to describe the social information that the child with autism is missing, like the context of a situation. Describing when a situation starts and finishes, what usually happens, and what people expect others to do and why can bring clarity and predictability and may immediately and dramatically reduce anxiety. Good examples of this are the Stories 'What is the plan for my school trip?' and 'What happens when there is a change of plan?' (page 265). Putting in place plenty of warning of change, and a visual timetable which concretely shows when lessons start and finish also supports the child and reduces anxiety.

Understanding language in school

Children with autism may have difficulty identifying the context of words. Words and phrases that are dependent on the context for their meaning may therefore be confusing and the child may not know when to take things literally or not. As a consequence, they struggle with understanding jokes and words or phrases that do not mean exactly what they say, such as metaphors, similes, idioms and sarcasm. It is surprising how much of our day-to-day language does not mean what it says! Language that depends on reading the social cues of body language, tone of voice or inflection on particular words for its intended meaning may likewise confuse the child who may not receive the intended meaning.

As children progress through school many different new skills and concepts are introduced to them, mostly in neurotypical language. Much of this language may be inaccessible for the very literal child and may cause confusion. A large number of Social Stories™ in this collection are written to explain a confusing phrase in a language the child can understand. Sometimes it is a misunderstood phrase that drives an unusual response and when this is clarified in a Social Story the response disappears. Some examples of Stories included here that explain the meaning of a word or phrase describing a skill or concept are: 'What is lining up?' (page 194) 'What is practice?' (page 83), 'What is revision?' (page 143) and 'What does "home" mean in a game?' (page 113).

How wonderful it would be if all introductions in school were in language that all our children could immediately understand!

Understanding other people in school

Friendships

As neurotypicals we are constantly aware of the thoughts, feelings, knowledge and beliefs of those around us, and those we are interacting with. This is called having a theory of mind. Again we do not have lessons in theory of mind, it just develops innately within us, and we cannot switch this process off. Having this ability allows us to be aware that we may be upsetting, annoying or boring another person and stimulates us to stop what we are doing, change topic or move away. This keeps us safe and effective in our interactions with other people.

Without theory of mind working well for him a child with autism may simply not have other people's thoughts and feelings in mind during his interactions with others. He may find it difficult or impossible to understand another's perspective of a situation or interaction. He may continue with a conversation for example, without taking turns to listen, unaware of the other person's upset or boredom, or he may state a fact about another child's appearance or performance that hurts their feelings. This makes it difficult for him to make and keep friendships.

Once focused in a one-to-one situation, and prompted with questions, he may be able to consciously work out what another person's feelings might be, but in the quickly moving social interaction there is no time for a thought-out response.

Waiting for a turn

Without the ability to have in mind what other people may be thinking, feeling or needing children with autism will most likely also have difficulty in situations where their needs are not immediately met. Being mindful of the needs and feelings of other children brings an understanding of the 'fairness' in waiting patiently for your turn. Without this information their perception may be, for example, that they need help now and that it is being withheld from them, resulting in a frustrated response. This is seen in the classroom where resources have to be shared and turns taken, for example with a classroom computer or even for the teacher's attention. An example of a Social Story™ sharing information about why a child needs to wait for the teacher's attention, with some suggestions on how to do it is: 'How to ask for help in the classroom' (page 72).

Asking questions for clarification

Being aware of other people's thoughts and knowledge also stimulates us to ask questions of them and to request help. Children with autism ask questions, sometimes repetitively for reassurance, but although frequently confused, they rarely ask someone to help them or clarify things for them. The reason for this may be their different theory of mind. They may be unaware of what other people know or assume other people know exactly what they know. They are unaware therefore that others may have solutions to the problem they are experiencing. So instead of asking for help they remain confused and solve their discomfort and confusion themselves, often in a practical way by leaving the situation or initiating removal from the uncomfortable situation or confusing task. Social Stories™ can describe what other people know and therefore why they can help, and a couple of examples in this collection would be: 'Who helps me in the classroom?' (page 72), 'What does my teacher know?'(page 93).

Reading other people's intentions

As a consequence of being unaware of what someone else knows or thinks, our young people may have difficulty in working out what someone's intention might be and whether it is friendly or unfriendly. With classmates this renders them extremely vulnerable to bullying. Examples of Stories sharing information about other children's intentions are: 'What is an intention?' and 'Who is in charge of the classroom?' (page 109).

Understanding negative directions in school

Negative commands are also frequently challenging for a child with autism because they require the child not only to understand what it is he is not to do, but also to know what alternative response is expected. This requires the child to use the context to make a good guess about what the teacher may be expecting here when they issue a negative direction. This is a task our children may struggle with due to a combination of lack of context sensitivity and of theory of mind, as described above.

For example, when a teacher points along a corridor and instructs the children standing in line beside her 'Don't run down the corridor!' a neurotypical child, using his ability to read context and theory of mind, guesses immediately what the teacher wants him to do in this situation and walks down the corridor. A child with autism may be less able or unable to make a good guess about either what the context is or what the adult is expecting. He may be confused by the command and signal and so may stand still, appearing less compliant or even defiant. He is actually doing what has been asked – he is not running down the corridor. The simple use of positive language in communicating with children with autism prevents this confusion. Directing children positively to 'Walk down the corridor' will, more often than not, result in a compliant response.

The special interest

Not every child with autism has a special interest but when they do have one it is a valuable source of relief for them and a valuable resource for us to connect with them. Within the neurotypical social world the child with autism may be confused and uncomfortable, but within his own world of his special interest he has absolute clarity and predictability. He is able to study it over and over again so he can read the emotions and even the intentions of the characters who usually display these clearly and graphically. It is a comfortable place to spend time, where he understands everything and knows exactly what will happen next.

Using language and examples from a special interest can be so helpful when we attempt to explain difficult emotions and intentions of others in the neurotypical world. Two examples of

Stories that do just this are: 'The story of Markachu II's chill attack' 'When to use my chill attack' (page 240) and 'What is a worthy opponent?' (page 230).

Social Stories™

It is very clear that children with autism have a different perspective of the world from their neurotypical peers, and their responses may seem unusual to us because of this difference. It is important to accept that their perspective is as valid to them as ours is to us. We need to respect this difference, find the missing information and share it with them. We can do so using the evidence-based, effective strategy of Social Stories.

A Social Story patiently describes the relevant clues in life, building and clarifying the context of a situation, sharing other people's thoughts, feelings and experiences and linking these to their reactions and expectations. It does so in a language that is always positive and literally accurate and therefore easily accessible for and respectful of the child with autism. It works hard to engage the child by considering his choice of interests and may incorporate illustrations that are meaningful for the child and which highlight the content of the Story. The result should be a uniquely meaningful, patient, non-judgmental, respectful and reassuring description of life.

Once the Story is shared two extraordinary things happen. First, nine times out of ten, the student's response changes as he has a new understanding of the situation, which he was unable to access before. Second, the more we strive to understand his perspective the more we come to see that nearly all his responses are just that – responses to a stimulus, not deliberate 'bad behaviour', defiance or manipulation. We find that we understand him more, just as he understands us more.

Carol Gray, the founder of the Social Stories™ approach, has defined ten criteria to guide safe and effective Social Story writing. These define what a Social Story is and the process that researches, writes and illustrates it. Following them ensures that the author writes a Story that is accessible, safe and effective for the individual child.

When the criteria are not kept in mind the neurotypical writer may inadvertently stray into a story that tells the child what to do, rather than finding and sharing the actual social information the child is missing. As a coach and trainer I have also met a few authors who have written Social Stories 'their way', disregarding the criteria and ending up with a written form of the verbal correction of the child that has already failed. These stories frequently are unsuccessful and cause further loss of self-esteem in the child. This may also lead to the rejection of the whole approach for that child, which is a great shame.

A guide to the criteria can be found in Carol Gray's recent book *The New Social Story™ Book* (2015) or on her website at www.carolgraysocialstories.com. All the Stories included in this collection were written following the ten criteria.

Introduction to Social Stories™ through the school years

Twenty-two years ago I heard Carol Gray speak about social understanding and the strategy of Social Stories™. I began to write them for my son who had been diagnosed with autism when he was 2 years old. I have continued to write them throughout his life. I am still writing them today, as the more grown up form, Social Articles. I was drawn to Carol's strategy because of her insight into the different, yet equally valid, perspective of the child with autism. Her respect for those with autism shone through her presentations and was evidenced by the patient, reassuring and respectful Stories she successfully shared with the children in her care. Right back then, in the early 1990s, Carol was talking from a platform of absolute respect for children with autism, not aiming to make them neurotypical, but rather discovering their perspective and sharing information with them, helping them to feel comfortable as themselves in an inhospitable world. This was quite unlike anything I had heard before. It made absolute sense to me. Twenty-two years later respect for the different perspective of the person with autism now underpins the professional opinion of all those working in the field. The evidenced-based Social Stories approach remains as cutting edge now as it was back then. It works!

A proactive description of life

Continually gathering information for my Stories led me to a deeper understanding of my child's perspective and changed me as well as improving his understanding. I began to write Stories proactively, not waiting for an unusual or undesired response to trigger the need for a solution in the form of a Social Story™. I wrote to explain everything that was going to happen, little changes and large. I wrote to explain about other people's lives and experiences. I wrote to describe what different emotions felt to him and how to self-regulate these. I described resilience skills such as self-reflection, positivity and flexibility. Each Story built on a previous Story, using illustrations that immediately brought to mind the content of a previous Story. I developed concepts Story by Story. All were, and still are, written in 'Social Story language', the language required for the child or young person to make information accessible.

And there is the nub. A neurotypical Mum teaches all these things seamlessly throughout a child's young life using their shared neurotypical language, assuming quite correctly that the child understands her language. My little chap was experiencing the world differently and spoke and understood another language. He was not receiving this information. Writing the Stories helped me focus my thoughts, understanding and choice of language into descriptions of life in Social Story language, which were literal, accurate and positive so that he would have equal access to this vital information. This resulted in a huge change in all my communication with him. Social Stories, I have discovered, have a profound communication effect on the author that continues long after the pencil is put down on the desk and, if they are used frequently enough, it eventually permeates the author's life.

With the use of this approach, and having it embedded in our family life, Mark was able to thrive. The proactive use of Stories to continuously describe life has helped replace confusion with understanding of himself, the world and other people. Many people, particularly professionals, use Social Stories™ solely to troubleshoot a 'challenging response', and this misses out on the full potential of this invaluable strategy.

Starting school: a change from proactive to reactive Stories

When Mark started school his daily context, during the school week, went beyond my reach. I could no longer see what was happening around him or hear what was being said or observe his responses or the responses of others to him. He was immersed in a world of complete and utter change. The people he met, although kind and well meaning, had different perspectives about autism from mine, interpreted his responses differently, and frequently used language that was inaccessible to him. Writing Stories for these situations was more challenging. Having spent years writing proactively I now had to write them reactively in response to reported 'behaviours' and to his increasing anxiety on return from school.

I was tremendously fortunate to have Helen Barker as his LSA. Helen willingly came along with me to be trained in autism and Social Stories so that she could bring some understanding of Mark's autism with him into school. I relied heavily on information gathered by Helen there. Occasionally I had access to school events that were open to the parents, such as sports day, swimming galas, school shows, assemblies and school outings. On these occasions I made lots of mental notes, which I rapidly scribbled down in a notebook to change into a Story when I got home.

I also gathered information from Mark as best I could, sometimes using drawing or Comic Strip Conversation or talking via a comfortable channel using his current special interest.

Using Comic Strip Conversations (Gray, 1994)

A Comic Strip Conversation (CSC) is a drawing conversation between a student and a parent or professional. Two people, paper, pens and privacy are all that is required! Its purpose is to provide insight into the child's perspective and share an alternative perspective with him. The conversation has a topic, usually a recent situation or interaction, which was either problematic for the child, or one in which they achieved a skill or demonstrated a response that deserves applause and recognition.

The conversation identifies where the event took place, which people were present, recalling what was said by whom, and in what order. People are represented by stick men drawings drawn initially by both parties but eventually predominantly by the student. The order in which the event happened is supported by open, unassuming guidance questions such as 'Where were you?' 'Who else was there?' 'What happened next?' 'What did you say?' 'What did others say?' These questions are initially required to help the student recall events in the social relevant sequence.

Spoken words that are normally transient (Hodgdon, 2013) are written inside speech bubbles and this allows the student with autism time to examine them and think about them – time that is not available within social interactions. The thoughts or intentions of others are also written inside thought bubbles. Guessing the thoughts or intentions of others is difficult for the student with autism and giving him time to re-examine his interpretation of another person's thoughts is very valuable. The student's perspective sometimes reveals a completely unexpected interpretation of the motivation or thoughts of other people. This opens up an opportunity for the neurotypical parent or professional to first acknowledge the student's perspective as valid and then respectfully draw and write an alternative suggestion.

Frequently the student then comes to his own conclusion that this may explain the outcome and this develops his understanding of the frequently baffling neurotypical perspective. The CSC may then go on to explore alternative safe and effective social responses and outcomes.

Colour may be used according to a colour chart chosen by the student. The colours identify the feelings behind words or thoughts and are used just in the speech and thought bubbles. An example might be green for 'friendly' and red for 'unfriendly'.

The information gained from a CSC frequently leads directly to a Social Story™ as it reveals the important social information that may be missing for the student. Personally speaking I am still being surprised by the different perspective a young person with autism has about the world. This technique is one of the most enlightening I have ever used and forms the basis for the majority of my Stories.

Maintaining engagement using the special interest

As Mark grew up his Stories needed to grow up with him. The social world was and is always going to be an uncomfortable place for him to spend a lot of time in. To share information about it I had to work hard to keep him continually engaged, particularly as he became a young adult.

The format of the Stories had to be continually respectful of his understanding, age and attention span so, as time went by, I initially changed the size of the font and included his growing vocabulary within longer sentences. Eventually the Stories took on a more formal style of font with more advanced vocabulary in an article format, called Social Articles. Mark continued to love the illustrations, which kept track with his interests, so these were included but were smaller in size and often without colour so they looked more adult. For many children the illustrations are an indication of a 'childish' book and sometimes a change to small black and white photographs placed strategically and sparsely in the Story can make a difference to engagement. I also used different media, using a tablet for one Story on fencing, and his mobile phone for a Story about safe travel. However, although variety may be the spice of life for those who are neurotypical, for some on the spectrum familiarity brings reassurance. At times of stress the old format (but with smaller font) was welcomed.

The most effective strategy to maintain engagement I have found is being respectful and *curious* about his interests, actively learning about them so that I can be articulate and knowledgeable about each subject. This has enabled us to continue to communicate well, enjoying each other's company. It has allowed me to select meaningful characters, phrases and images taken from the world he chooses to immerse himself in, and use these to describe more difficult perseverative concepts like winning and losing. Let me share one example. Morgan Freeman narrates the film *March of the Penguins*. Mark has watched this film hundreds of times. In the film, the Emperor penguin chicks, while still quite young, are taken by their parent and left in a penguin 'crèche' with all the other chicks while their parent goes to find food. In one particularly touching scene a chick refuses to stay and tries to follow its parent. Its parent gently but firmly nudges it back to the crèche. Morgan narrates in his very distinctive voice 'For some this is unacceptable…but, non-negotiable.' Mark copied this phrase immediately in Morgan's exact accent. It clearly struck a chord with him. Because we watched the film together I noted this. I felt quite sure that had the scene involved humans rather than penguins he would have been unable to read the emotions. The penguins, lacking facial expression and language, showed their distress much more clearly by their actions, and being able to watch this over and over clarified exactly what was happening. We then talked about how it sometimes felt to be dropped at school and how similar this might be to how the penguin chick felt.

Now I had a phrase that I could use for Mark to instantly recall that although some things are challenging, sometimes the challenge has to be faced and got through as comfortably as possible. Like Temple Grandin, he thinks in pictures (Grandin, 2006), so when he hears the phrase he has an immediate vision of the penguin scene. He also recalls that the parent returns with food and the separation is temporary. Mark and I have used this phrase again and again over the years, but only for uncomfortable challenges that he absolutely has to face. Many years later dropping him to his apprenticeship workplace he said the phrase, with a sad smile, as he got out of the car. He did not need to explain any further – I knew exactly what he was feeling and was able to immediately reassure him that I would pick him up at the usual time.

I have learned about many different special interests over the years, including Japanese anime, Cosplay, Duel Monsters, meerkats, penguins, and the TV programme *Top Gear*. These were subjects I would not have chosen myself but when I became familiar with them I was always surprised by what they told me about Mark, his feelings and experiences, and over time I became very fond of them too because they connected me with him.

Maintaining engagement using the power of praise Stories

As Mark grew up, the need to maintain self-esteem also continued to grow and I found the power of praise Stories here really helped to develop positive self-reflection and a positive outlook. Fifty per cent of all Stories should be written praising the child about a current skill or achievement to build self-esteem. Sadly, parents and professionals frequently tell me that it takes so much time and energy to write one Story addressing a pressing problem that the praise Story applauding an achievement often gets neglected. This is a great shame because writing praise Stories focuses not just the child but also the parent or professional on his positive achievements and attributes. A lot of attention is focused on what the child is struggling with and therefore actively thinking about what the child currently does well can reframe the parent's or professional's understanding of the whole child in a much more positive way. It can also direct the professional to look at situations in school when the child is engaged and learning. This may stimulate a reappraisal of what supportive environment present in that situation could be facilitating this. Most importantly, the praise Story builds the child's self-esteem.

Time was frequently short for me too, and when I could not write a full praise Story, I would write what I called a 'praise comment'. This was a short documentation of the positive comments made by others about a particular quality, skill or achievement. I would write down the name of the person, recording the date and place and then their exact words, in a way similar to the Captain's Log Star Date in *Star Trek*! Each comment, sometimes on its original piece of paper, was then stuck in a notebook to compile a bank of positive praise. Sometimes I wrote a praise comment inside a congratulations card. These praise comments became a valuable resource to Mark and a valuable resource for me too – seeing in print the great things other people have said about my son still reinvigorates me on a low day!

As all young people grow up, praise from parents becomes less valid to them. They may even reject it. The most powerful praise Stories in the older school age group are the ones written by a staff member, a peer or an older student. Praise from others outside the family is much more powerful and so praise comments also work remarkably well as children move into adolescence and beyond. An example of one of these was, 'Mr U... on 5th February, 2011 at ... College, "I love teaching Mark. His focus is amazing! I wish I had a classful like him".'

The comment, partly because of its brevity, was usually quite specific. In the example above the college tutor praises Mark's *focus*. This is much less patronising than, for example, praising his good behaviour.

Sometimes when I had more time I would return to the comment and write a full Social Story™ around it, meanwhile Mark had received an immediate injection of positive praise!

In his last year at school Helen, his LSA, compiled a similar book *full* of comments by staff who were happy to contribute. Each comment focused on something they liked and would remember about Mark. Some were even illustrated. This incredible collection of 'praise comments' has been used to build self-esteem on many, many occasions since and will always be treasured by him.

To introduce a praise Story Carol Gray suggests using this phrase, 'Yesterday I saw you do something amazing. It was so amazing I had to write it down' then producing the praise Story for the child to read. This can be used in the same way with a praise comment. This is a highly effective way to introduce praise. For a young person who rejects direct affirmation, deliberately allowing him to overhear praise may be a more effective way of delivering it.

Developing Resilience with Social Stories

There is a great deal of current interest focusing on the well-being and mental health of young people with autism in response to the high incidence of depression and anxiety within those with an autism spectrum condition (ASC). In particular, professionals are looking for effective ways to help our young people with autism develop resilience, beginning early in their school lives. Resilience is the ability to bounce back from adversity, to weather the storms of life without slipping into despondency and depression. Resilient people are noted to be optimists, seeing the positive side to a negative situation, to be flexible to change, to have the capability to self-reflect and empathise as well as having the support of a network of friends. All of these qualities are compromised for the young person with autism. The Social Story™ approach addresses all of these areas and, with consistent work on an individual basis, I believe it is possible with Social Stories to help a young person develop a more resilient skill set, starting early in childhood, and continuing through school education into adulthood. How do they do this?

Social Stories build positivity

Social Stories always strive to be positive and reassuring, actively avoiding negative vocabulary and never ever describing an undesired response in the first person, but rather describing a positive, safe and effective alternative response. Fifty per cent of all Stories are required to be praise Stories, applauding the skills and achievements of those with autism, and praise comments can augment this. Continually writing Social Stories therefore naturally redresses the balance between positivity and negativity.

Social Stories build flexibility

Flexibility to changing context is a huge challenge for people with autism. A Social Story describes the context of each situation in detail, guided by six questions: When is it happening? Where is it happening? Who is there? What happens? How does it happen? Why does it happen? Going on further to describe similar contexts in different situations using a Story as a master copy then builds not only generalisation but also transferrable skills and flexibility. This is amplified by Stories focusing on how a young person has successfully managed changes throughout their life. When the young person is armed with specific individual self-regulation behaviours described in Social Stories™, and encouraged in the face of changes, surprising flexibility emerges.

Social Stories help and encourage self-reflection

Social Stories encourage self-reflection by using social information from the past combined with the present, to take forward into the future. This allows the young people to reflect on past challenges they have overcome and thereby develop an understanding of their potential to overcome future challenges. This builds self-esteem, confidence and courage to take on the next challenge building perseverance.

Social Stories build empathy

Empathy may be thought of as the ability to share and understand the feelings of another person. To be empathic first requires information about another person's internal state. The goal of every Social Story is to share accurate information about the social world. This includes the thoughts, feelings, experiences and beliefs of others. Once armed with information about another person's feelings from a Social Story the child or adult with autism may express empathy to the same degree as a neurotypical and in many cases to a far greater degree!

Social Stories encourage sociability

Using information that has been carefully gathered, each Social Story shares the missing social information with the young person. A coaching sentence may be included to gently guide him towards a safe and effective response. Sometimes a phase or words are suggested too. With this information the young person with autism is empowered to embrace a social situation with more 'tools' and understanding, and therefore may be more successful socially. This builds confidence and encourages him to enter the social arena when he wishes to.

Each Story in this book has an introduction which sets the scene and describes the different perspective of the young person with autism within that school setting, explaining what social information was missing and how it was uncovered. This is then followed by a Social Story™, which was used with Mark and others and had a successful outcome. It is important to note that the illustrations I have used throughout were meaningful for Mark and may not be for another young person with autism. The Stories are arranged according to topic, not in chronological order, so Stories for primary and secondary school-aged students will be side by side, often sharing a common introduction.

Mark and I feel very privileged to have had the Social Stories approach as a powerful and loyal partner as we have navigated our way together through the social world for the last 22 years. We hope that by sharing our successful examples of Stories written for the school years, your understanding of autism will deepen and broaden, and that you may be inspired to learn more about this wonderful approach, using it to describe life for your young person through school and into adulthood and beyond.

The Classroom

Stories about growing up
I am still growing up
My teacher grew up too

In the school setting there are many new skills to learn, the majority of which will be learned in small steps with plenty of practice. A good deal of patience and perseverance are required to do this. What allows most children and adults to persevere with a sometimes daunting task, when there is slow or little progress, is the understanding that they have accomplished difficult things before over time.

Children with autism may have poor episodic memory, which means they struggle to recall their own past personal experiences (Bowler, Gardiner and Grice, 2000; Goddard *et al.*, 2014). Episodic memory is important because it provides us with a sense of personal history, contributing to our autobiographical memory. In terms of having the confidence to persevere with a challenging task we often draw on our episodic memory to recall how we have achieved success in the past. Without this ability the child with autism may be less able to be mindful of his own successes and may instead focus on more recent failures.

Social Stories™ can help here to make this self-reflection feasible by effectively combining the past, present and future tenses together in one Story, reminding the child in a concrete and permanent way of his past successes. This is also critically important in developing resilience skills.

Earlier in Mark's childhood I wrote a Social Story™ 'I am growing up' to redress this imbalance, which concretely demonstrated to Mark that as he grew up and transitioned between the early stages of life he was achieving success – he had learned how to sit, to walk, to run, to push a train and so on. It emphasised that he was growing up not just in size but also in achievements. This lifespan Story became the foundation to many Stories that have helped him, and others, understand their own progress and encouraged them to try new experiences. Even if a child does not achieve physical milestones at the same time as others, there is nearly always some progress that can be highlighted from his early years. This topic was revisited in the following Story 'I am still growing up', which describes how the child is on a continuing journey of development towards adulthood, which makes sense of learning new skills and taking on new responsibilities.

School years are a time of change for the child's body as they physically develop into an adolescent. Reflecting on the changes their bodies have already gone through as they grew from baby to toddler to child helps highlight that at each stage of life the body changes in order to equip it for the next stage.

The child with autism may be unaware that the adults in his life have experienced childhood and adolescence too, which requires mindfulness of others' experiences using theory of mind, which is working less well for him. The second Story included here describes that just as the child has grown up and is continuing to grow up, his teacher once grew up too. This provides social information around the teacher's life experience, which builds the foundation for the later Story 'What does my teacher know?' By understanding that the teacher grew up too, the child gains information about growing up which may be helpful if he is struggling with adolescence. To produce this Story obviously requires the teacher to be understanding and co-operative and also to be happy to provide photos! They may also need to be prepared to help the child with any questions around growing up.

I am still growing up

I am 12 years old and I am still growing up. I have been a baby and I have been a child. I am now an older child and soon I will become a teenager.

When babies become children their body changes. This is part of normal growing up. Changes in the body help babies learn to walk, run and develop new fun skills like riding a bike, skateboarding or swimming.

As children become teenagers their bodies change again too. This is okay. These changes in the body help them get ready to be a young adult.

Becoming a young adult brings many new fun privileges and also some responsibilities. As children grow they become teenagers and then become young adults. This is a normal part of growing up.

I have been a baby and I have been a child. I am now an older child and soon I will become a teenager. One day I will be a young adult. I am still growing up and this is okay.

My teacher grew up too

Mr T is usually my teacher. When Mr T was born he was a baby. Mr T grew and became a child. Here is a picture of Mr T when he was 6 years old.

Mr T grew and became a teenager. Here is a picture of Mr. T when he was a teenager. In this picture he is about 13 years old.

Mr T grew and became a young man and now he is an adult. Here is a picture of Mr T as an adult.

Mr T has been a baby, a child, a teenager, a young man and now is an adult. My teacher, Mr T, grew up too.

I am learning to listen
to the teacher

Children and young adults with autism often struggle to make themselves comfortable in our world. Because of their different social understanding they may not ask for help but instead seek resolution themselves. This is mainly because they may not be mindful that others have knowledge or experience that is different to their own. This frequently results in them displaying an unusual social response which can be labelled a 'behaviour'. I have learned that there is a huge amount of information to be gained from observing the child and their response, and then questioning how they are experiencing the situation and why their response alleviates it for them. This then leads me to understanding their perspective better and helps me write more effective Social Stories™. Sometimes it leads me to a solution that is more sensory focused and a Story is not even required!

Mark, like many other children and young adults with autism, frequently avoids looking at the area of the face around the eyes. High functioning people with autism have described this sensation as uncomfortable or even unbearable. They frequently describe that in order to listen rather than looking at the speaker they need to look at a plain or unstimulating surface, like the floor or a wall. So for some, discomfort may be the reason they avoid eye contact. For others, it may be that looking at someone's face is pointless because they do not receive useful social information from doing so, or perhaps they do not know that they are expected to do so.

Looking at the speaker to show attention is an important skill in school, college and the workplace. Without this skill a student may appear to be disinterested and switched off in a world of his own, when in fact he is actively trying to pay full attention. Teaching staff frequently mention that the student is not paying attention when he is staring out of the window or at the floor. Sometimes the student will be asked to look at the teacher or parent to show he is listening. However, looking at the adult may render the student incapable of listening at all. The most common time a student is requested to look at a teacher or parent's face may be when he has done something perceived as wrong and needing correction. Frequently this is accompanied therefore by a raised voice and a stern facial expression. The result may be overwhelming for him.

Once Mark was able to tell me he found eye contact 'uncomfy' (his term for uncomfortable) this Story was written to validate the sensation he was feeling, acknowledge the difficulty this posed him and find a compromise that was respectful of this, but also sharing information on what others need to know. Describing looking at the teacher for a short time then looking away helped him remain comfortable while showing the teacher that he was listening. Asking him to count to three 'penguins' allowed about 3 seconds to elapse. As penguins were a special interest they were comforting to think about. Sharing the Story with the staff involved was a very valuable way of explaining Mark's different perception of the situation and this also helped improve their understanding of his autism.

Although the original Story started with Mum as the person he was learning to listen to, for school and college this was replaced by the 'teacher' then the 'tutor'. This used the original Story as a master copy, a Story Master, from which other Stories, in a similar format, could be made to build generalisation of the skill of listening to different adults in different settings.

Many years later, while working on interview skills in the hunt for an apprenticeship, we used the Story again as a Story Master, replacing 'teacher' this time with 'interviewer' and including detail about what the interviewer knew about Mark and the apprenticeship he was being interviewed for.

It is important to realise that although this Story may appear repetitive to neurotypicals, for some children with autism the repetitive nature of the format is reassuring and familiar, and in a world where it is hard to predict what is going to happen or what someone is going to say, this may be comforting. Of course, for higher functioning young people the repetitive format may feel childish, so effort must go in to individualising the Story for the young person. A Social Story™ should always be written at the child's exact cognitive level, with the format, sentence length and vocabulary chosen specifically for the individual child. Keeping this in mind at all times helps to prevent the child feeling patronised or challenged by a Story. Moving towards a Social Article format as they grow is important to prevent disengagement with the technique.

I am learning to listen to the teacher

Listening is an important skill to learn. I am learning how to listen to the teacher. My class teacher is usually Mrs R.

Mrs R knows lots of things to tell me. Mrs R knows how to keep me safe. She knows good stories too! Mrs R knows I am listening when I am looking at her.

Sometimes I may find it uncomfy to look at Mrs R's face. Mrs R understands that this may be uncomfy for me. Mrs R and I have made a plan to keep me comfy. This is okay.

I may look at her for just a short time (count to three penguins) and then look away. In a little while I may look at her again.

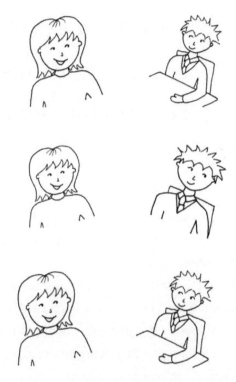

Looking for a short time and then looking away from someone's face is called 'glancing'. I have already learned to glance at Mum and Dad. I am learning to glance at Mrs R.

When Mrs R talks to me I will try to glance at her face. Then Mrs R will know I am listening and I may feel comfy. Mrs R will be pleased with me.

Stories about calm
What is calm for me?
What does calm down mean?
How to ask for chill out time

Children with autism struggle with identifying emotions and feelings in others. They also struggle with identifying emotions and feelings within themselves. Identifying physical sensations inside our bodies and making sense of them allows us to recognise when we feel different emotional states such as frightened, calm, angry or surprised. It also allows us to distinguish hunger from feeling too full, or discomfort from pain. Identifying and recognising our own emotional or physical internal state triggers us to self-regulate and, in the case of pain or illness, to seek help.

This may not be working optimally for a child with autism, who may be unable to recognise even what the simple state of 'calm' feels like for him. Consequently, requests from teaching staff to 'calm down' when he is anxious or agitated may therefore hold no meaning for him at all. He will be unable to reach a calm state if he does not know where or what it is and how to get himself there.

However, like Mark, each and every day the child will be finding 'calm' using his own methods of self-regulation to do so. At school, walking the perimeter fence up and down is self-regulating, as is a quiet time in the reading corner looking at a familiar book, or drawing the same picture over and over again. At home when slumped comfortably on a beanbag watching his special interest of penguins on a DVD over and over again, he is self-regulating. When he repetitively feels a particular hanky between his fingers or listens to his music over and over again through headphones he is self-regulating, helping himself to feel better.

It is important therefore that the child is helped to recognise that the feeling he experiences while indulging in these self-sought strategies is called 'calm'. Commenting in a positive way when the child is observed to be calm is a first step. I used the phrase, 'You look safe and comfy, Mark. I am guessing you are feeling calm' and then I took a photo of each scenario, placing the photos in a small book which we would then look at from time to time together. I did not take photos of when he was excited or happy because these states were not calm! The 'calm' book was not used as a therapeutic resource but a method of raising his awareness of what calm felt like for him. I then used the pictures to write a Social Story™ describing these activities and then describing how others liked being around him when he was calm. I have included a version of this Story here called 'What is calm for me?', which was originally written for the home environment but has been adapted here for school.

The second Story 'How to calm down in school' goes on to describe what 'calm down' means and how to do it, using some of his own soothing strategies adapted for when away from home in school. Again this was originally written for home and has been adapted here for the school environment.

It also shared knowledge that he was missing about other people – that we all feel anxious or worried at times and we all feel calm sometimes. We all have our own individual methods of calming ourselves down too. A cup of tea, several deep breaths, a walk in the corridor, or just popping outside for some fresh air – we all have personal, effective strategies that we use to self-regulate and keep ourselves feeling comfortable. To support the Story at home, family members stated when they were feeling worried or anxious and how they were going to calm themselves down. I role-played my 'cup of tea' strategy with emphasis so it was clear that I too employed a calming strategy. A teacher or LSA can also model their strategy for the child in school.

To describe how to 'calm down', the child's own soothing strategies need to be made more portable so that they can be accessed away from home in the school environment. Although ideally this work is best started at home, where most of his calming activity is based, it can also be done at school. The calming effect from walking the perimeter fence or feeling a comfort object or fabric, or whatever calming strategy the child employs, can be commented on and photographed. Once these have been identified and recognised, the teacher or parent, and preferably both collaboratively, can adapt the calming techniques to be portable. The important thing I believe is to use techniques that the child has already shown by his own choice to be effective for him.

For Mark a piece of his hanky, which he liked to feel between his fingers, could be safely taken out and about sewn inside his trouser pocket. Permanently fixing it there prevented it being lost or laughed at by peers. This can be done for most students with autism in the classroom in a similar way. Parents identifying their child's need to feel something between their fingers have sewn fur fabric, Velcro, small keyrings of lego or magnets inside the child's pocket with great success. Students feel very comforted knowing this source of calm is there all the time.

Listening to music through headphones could be adapted using smaller portable earphones. Giving the student access to this at playtime may allow him to calm himself and feel relaxed. Some computer games that are favourites of children have soundtracks that are comforting and can be downloaded and listened to in order to self-regulate, for example Minecraft, which many children with autism find calming, if only for its familiarity.

For Mark a favourite penguin DVD at home was converted to the portable and instant strategy of counting to ten penguins in his mind, or sequentially naming the different kinds of penguin in height order. Counting alone was not sufficiently calming, but counting penguins was something completely different and a step into his special interest – a really comfy place to be! Another special interest in a Japanese video game allowed him to identify with the most diplomatic and pacifist character and call to mind how he tackled an unexpected situation in the game. This was of course researched first to make sure the character reacted in a calm way!

Sometimes a strategy may be specific for a particular stress environment. Mark used to become physically tense during spelling tests and exams. Helen, his LSA, on noticing his hunched, tense shoulders would remind him to 'let your shoulders go loose' which allowed his body to relax and helped his anxiety. She developed many novel relaxation techniques that helped him during his school years.

Staying current with the child's special interests allows the strategies to be adapted so that they are always meaningful for the child at whatever age they are. Simply seeing the drawing of the strategy may allow him to recall it, so it was useful to embed the illustration within a Story to add extra meaning.

To illustrate the following Stories in this book, I have used the original calming strategies of the hanky in the pocket, penguin counting and thinking of a special interest character, adding in the 'shoulders down' technique and thinking about an episode of Danger Mouse as an alternative character to think about. Over time, as he grew older, Mark developed and used many other interests and strategies of his own.

The third Story in this set of Stories, 'How to ask for chill out time', was originally written for the home environment and was not needed for Mark in school. However, it is included here because sometimes a child needs to access restorative isolation in a quiet place when feeling overwhelmed at school. Because of his different theory of mind, a child with autism may not think to ask to do so. Occasionally he may learn that a certain undesired behaviour will access the same outcome and therefore it is necessary to introduce the safer and more socially effective method of using a phrase or card. The Story explains the need to use the phrase so that others understand his need. Knowing that there is a refuge in the sometimes inhospitable school world can reassure a young person with autism considerably.

Within the 'How to calm down in school' Story I describe the employment of Mark's strategies 'when unexpected things happen'. I did not ask him to employ them when *anxious,* because he was not always able to work out when he was feeling anxious. Identifying unexpected things, however, was his specialty and, once seen, these unexpected things usually led to anxiety, so this was a good starting point to begin using his calming tools.

Once these Stories were implemented and the concept had both meaning and a comforting strategy attached to it, I was able also to make reference to them in other Social Stories™ using the coaching sentence 'I will try to stay calm', which now had extra practical meaning as he had a sensory tool (his hanky), a cognitive tool (thinking about ten penguins), and an escape tool (asking for chill out time) within his reach at all times. He was beginning to build his own portable and immediately accessible self-regulation toolbox (Attwood, 2008).

Several parents have shared with me that making a similar 'calm book' for their child has helped provide some cherished moments looking at it together. The Stories have frequently been requested for other children and have been used successfully after being appropriately individualised for them. I am always careful, however, to make sure anyone considering using this Story as a template for a child has understood that when using the first person to describe a child's emotional state the author must be very, very careful that the feeling he describes as the child's own feeling is accurate from *the perspective of the child*, and not make assumptions from his own neurotypical perspective, or describe how he wishes the child to feel. This is particularly important in school where Stories are more often used in a troubleshooting way around an undesired and challenging response. It is easy in this circumstance to slip into telling the child that he feels calm when his body is still and he is quiet, which of course is what the author wishes he would do. In reality this child may need to move or feel something between his fingers in order to feel calm, and if he complies with the request his anxiety will catapult up. The Social Story™ approach requires us to find and share social information that is *accurate and meaningful for the child*, leading to improved understanding so that the child can choose a safer and more effective response.

What is calm for me?

Feeling calm is a good feeling. Feeling calm is a comfy safe feeling. Many people like to feel calm. I usually feel calm at home when I feel my hanky.

Sometimes I feel calm at home when I think about penguins or watch my penguin DVD.

At school I usually feel calm when I read my book in the quiet room.

Sometimes at break time I feel calm when I listen to my music with my headphones.

Other times at break time I feel calm when I walk along beside the playground fence. This is okay.

Feeling calm is a good feeling. Feeling calm is a comfy, safe feeling. Other children like being around me when I am feeling calm.

I am learning about what calm is for me.

What does calm down mean?

Sometimes children feel calm. Sometimes children feel worried. Many children and adults feel worried some of the time and calm some of the time. This is okay.

Usually when someone is worried they try to make themselves feel calmer. This is called 'calming down'. People try to 'calm down' because feeling calm is a good comfy feeling.

People usually have a favourite way of calming down.

My LSA takes three big breaths when she needs to calm down. This helps her think clearly when unexpected things happen.

I am learning how to calm down. Learning how to calm down may help me think clearly when unexpected things happen. Four things that may help me calm down are:

1. Counting to ten penguins

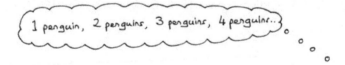

2. Thinking about an episode of Danger Mouse

3. Feeling my hanky in my pocket

4. Asking for chill out time

I will work on calming down when unexpected things happen. My teacher and my LSA will be pleased with me.

How to ask for chill out time

Sometimes I feel happy to be with other people.

Other times I want to be in a quiet place alone. This is okay. Everyone feels like this sometimes.

A good place to have quiet time alone at school is in the quiet room. My teacher, my LSA and I call having time in the quiet room 'chill out time'.

My teacher, LSA and my classmates know that it is important for me to have quiet time on my own sometimes. When I need quiet time alone at school I may say, 'I need to chill out' and go to the quiet room.

I need to chill out

Having quiet time alone helps me to reset. When I feel better I can come back.

Saying 'I need to chill out' lets other people know how I am feeling.

I will try to remember to say, 'I need to chill out' when I need to have quiet time alone. My teacher, my LSA and my classmates will understand.

Stories about help in the classroom

Who helps me in the classroom?

How to ask for help in the classroom

Children with autism are frequently assigned an LSA to help them with their learning and also to facilitate getting along with their peers. This role is a crucial one for the comfort of the child and may make all the difference between a child succeeding or failing in their placement within mainstream education. Dean Beadle, a young adult with Asperger syndrome who is an acclaimed international speaker and journalist, recognises that his LSA was the only person who truly understood his perspective and helped him manage himself during his school years. He remains, as a young working adult, still in touch with her to this day.

Mark was very fortunate too to have Helen Barker as his LSA. Helen first met Mark when he was transitioning between the autism resource unit at his special school, Market Field School, and mainstream primary school. Initially she sat in on his time at the special school and transferred gradually to the primary school with him, initially one day a week, building up to full-time attendance. Helen helped Mark feel that with her help there was nothing he could not at least attempt, and that nothing would be allowed to become unbearable for him on her watch. She had his back, was his safe house, she understood him and could read his responses very well. This did not happen by accident. Helen was open and willing to learn about autism and accompanied me on different training sessions and conferences, many in her own time, including the Social Story™ training with Carol Gray. She listened to me as a parent and valued my opinion. This made our communication about Mark very effective and incredibly safe for him. Helen also modelled how to interact with him positively for new staff and other children. They had a lot of fun and laughter together and this showed Mark's qualities at their best to staff who may have felt anxious about their new student. Mark and Helen developed a very close, trusting relationship which has lasted and still remains strong. Helen became a dear friend and will always be an important part of our family.

When Helen was not available, Mark had another LSA called Sandra. Sandra was also someone who was immensely caring and helped Mark tremendously. When Helen was away, which happened very rarely, Sandra was always a reassuring person to have at his side.

Not all students are so fortunate. Sometimes children are assigned LSAs who have had little or no training in autism. Their role becomes one of 'caretaker' rather than advocate and facilitator. More training is becoming available nowadays across all sectors of education and I am seeing great improvements in the awareness and understanding of autism in school staff.

However, there is still a lack of explanation to the child about who the LSA is, what the initials LSA mean, what an LSA knows, how they will support the child and how to ask them for help.

A home visit by the LSA to get to know the child where he is most relaxed and doing the things that engage and comfort him is really helpful and gets the relationship off to a good start. This helps build trust between the child and the LSA and is time well spent. Building trust is critical if the relationship is going to work well.

In order to access help in the classroom, the child needs to know how to ask for help and how to wait patiently for it to arrive. Waiting patiently is an important skill that requires the child to stay calm while waiting for his turn. This is difficult for children with autism because they are not mindful of the needs of other children due to their theory of mind differences. I also needed to share with Mark the important information that an adult could only help one child at a time, information that requires the ability to be mindful of the adult's abilities and thoughts, and finally I described specific calming tools that had been identified as working well for the child, and already chosen by them, to help stay calm while waiting for help (see page 73).

In school, the concept needs to be further generalised from waiting patiently for attention from Mum into waiting patiently for attention from the teacher or LSA. To do this, the original Story format was revisited and adapted to fit the classroom situation. This re-use of a Story format as a Story Master is an effective way of generalising a skill into a different context.

The first Social Story™ that follows here was written at a primary school level to describe who helps the child in the classroom. The second Story was written to share information on raising the hand to ask for help, a simple task that a child may never have met before in the home, but which is so important for the classroom. Another Story was written at a secondary school level to describe the role of an LSA to a student (page 105).

Using the Social Story™ as an approach rather than a single troubleshooting strategy allows us to use Stories to describe life *before* it becomes problematic for our students. I hope these following Stories will help parents and professionals to proactively describe the LSA role to their child before they run into misunderstandings.

Who helps me in the classroom?

Children go to school to learn new things. Sometimes learning new things is easy and happens straight away. Sometimes children need help to understand and learn.

Mrs T is usually my class teacher.

Mrs B is usually my learning support assistant. A learning support assistant may also be called an LSA for short.

Mrs B knows about me and knows how to help me understand and learn. Mrs B knows how to help me get along with other children too.

It is the teacher's job and the LSA's job to help children learn and to help children get along together too.

When I need help I may ask Mrs B or the teacher. Mrs B will be pleased to help me.

I am learning about help in the classroom.

How to ask for help in the classroom

Children go to school to learn new things. Sometimes learning new things is easy and happens straight away. Sometimes children need help to understand and learn. To ask for help in the classroom a child usually raises his hand.

This lets the teacher or LSA know that he needs help.

The teacher or LSA usually responds as soon as she can.

The teacher or LSA can only help one child at a time. Other children may need help too. Sometimes a child has to wait patiently until it is his turn.

I will try to raise my hand to ask for help and wait patiently until it is my turn.

To wait patiently I may use my calming tools. I may:

Count penguins

Think about an episode of Danger Mouse

Feel my hanky in my pocket

Write down what I want to ask

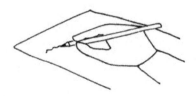

My teacher or LSA will help when she is ready. When she comes to help me I may put my hand down. I am learning about asking for help in the classroom.

What is practice?

Without the innate ability to self-reflect, Mark often found it difficult to recall skills in the past that had required a lot of practice to establish. This hampered his understanding of the importance of practice and perseverance. As a result, he would quickly become frustrated when he did not immediately become competent at a new skill. He is not alone here and many other parents over the years have shared with me that their children also experience this frustration. Exploring his perspective with a Comic Strip Conversation allowed Mark to explain to me that he felt it was unfair that he could not do a skill when he had the same kit as another child who could!

Neurotypicals know that simply buying the kit for football does not give children the ability to play football at a high standard. We are aware of the likely ability, experience and training of another child, particularly if they are displaying excellent skills. We understand that it is the underlying physical ability and then continued practice of the skill over time that has built the skill. Without the ability to be mindful of another's experience, however, there is a lack of information about what the other child's experience might have been, including how long they had been learning and practising the sport. This can lead to frustration for the child with autism when he is unable to achieve the same success immediately.

So there was need to share this missing information in a Social Story™. First I explained what the word practice meant. Then I concretely recorded the skills that Mark had achieved, only after lots of practice, in the past. These events were skills that he was proud of and still used, in order for the Story to be meaningful and engaging for him now. The subsequent Story allowed him to see that with practice he could improve, and together with his personal best book strategy and Story (page 234), he could become *the best he could be* at any sport or skill, within the classroom or on the sports ground. It also shared that all people need to practise new skills, even Mum!

Of course, this Story does not address the fact that different people are born with different strengths and talents that allow them to achieve excellence in sports and academic subjects, so this was addressed in a separate Story, with clear examples of both Mark's and others' unique strengths.

Social Stories™ often use references to time, which neurotypicals may assume the child understands simply because they are innately obvious to us. For example, in this Story I refer to 'less often'. It is extremely important that as authors we make sure the child has a good understanding of these phrases and that we only use ones that the child *currently* understands. I use a time line with 'always' at the top and 'never' on the bottom, and Mark and I discuss where to place new time phrases between these two extremes as we come across them (Gray, 2015). Without this supporting background work and careful selection of phrases related to time, the sentence 'mistakes happening less often' would not have been a clear concept. The same applies to the idea of 'more and more' compared to 'fewer and fewer'. It is important that the accuracy and the child's understanding of all the vocabulary being chosen for the Stories is continually checked and never assumed.

Another example is the phrase 'again and again'. I wanted to use the phrase 'over and over' here but Mark did not understand or use this phrase. Instead I chose 'again' because I knew that this was a word he often used and understood, so I could use it here with confidence. Parents and professionals wanting to use my examples of Stories for their children need to check their individual child's understanding of these phrases before reviewing the Stories with them.

I always checked with Mark that he understood the meaning of the words I wanted to use in a Story, and if he was unclear, I would consult an age-appropriate (his cognitive not chronological age) dictionary and a thesaurus to supply me with alternatives. Sometimes if a word was really important to use in the Story I built his understanding of the word first, writing about what it meant, before using it in another Story. Occasionally this involved actually taking him out to experience something that, because of his difficulties, he had not already experienced. I am always determined that when I present him with a Social Story™ describing the confusion of life that I use autism-friendly language, which is of course Social Story language, so that my words add only improved clarity and predictability to his world.

What is practice?

When I was a baby I crawled. As I grew older I wanted to walk. I tried again and again to walk. Trying again and again to improve a new skill is called practice. After lots and lots of practice I learned to walk!

When I was 4 years old I could walk, run and hop. I wanted to ride a scooter. I kept trying again and again to ride my scooter. I practised and practised. After lots and lots of practice I learned to ride my scooter. I can ride my scooter to the park now!

When I started swimming lessons I could only splash in the water. I wanted to swim. I practised and practised in my swimming lessons. After lots of practice I can swim a width now without armbands!

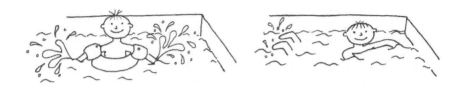

Two years ago Mum wrote her Stories with a pen on paper. Mum wanted to use a computer to write them. She practised and practised on the computer. After lots of practice Mum learned to use the computer. Mum writes all her Stories on the computer now!

Children and adults usually have to practise to improve new skills. When practising something new everyone makes mistakes. This is okay. As children and adults practise more and more they usually make fewer and fewer mistakes. Practice helps mistakes happen less often.

Some new things I can do straight away; some new things I may need to practise.

I am learning about practice.

What is a spelling test?

Young people with autism may have extremely high expectations of themselves academically. This may lead to perfectionism where good is never good enough and excellent or 'the best' is the only result worth having. Probably the first test children face in primary school is a spelling test, and this is often where teachers first witness a child's distressed response when he fails to achieve 10/10.

Sometimes reflection on the words we use to introduce the concept of a spelling test can reveal a possible misunderstanding by the very literal child with autism of the inferred meaning of our words. Teachers may say, 'I want you to work on your spellings at home this week and get 10/10 on Monday' or, 'When you get 10/10 for your spellings you will have a star.'

The child who is neurotypical understands this is not an absolute, that 9/10 is a very good score and that 10/10 is to be aimed at, but maybe not always achieved. But to the child with autism, achieving 10/10 is the complete and only purpose of sitting the test, as stated by the teacher! He may be unable to think what the teacher may feel about a score that is less than perfect because of his different theory of mind.

Mark always wanted to get his spellings right and struggled when some were marked wrong. Despite many reassurances that 8/10 was a very good score, he was not reassured. I think this may be the case for many of our children. The teacher or parent's first statement of introduction sets the bar and subsequent remarks and reassurances are often seen as less valid.

So the following Story simply describes when the spelling test usually happens, what happens and what the purpose of the test is. I included very important information about how staying calm helps his brain remember the spellings and reminded him of his own already established and effective calming tools. After reviewing the Story I shared Tony Attwood's remarks about calmness improving the recovery of solutions: 'If you remain calm you remain smart' (Attwood, 2008).

Simple though this Story is, it is full of really crucial information around spelling tests that may be obvious to many children but is not always there for many children with autism. There is no discussion of the negative feelings of disappointment here, only gentle guidance to positive ways to help the score. This, combined with the idea of the purpose of the test being to identify spellings that need more attention, seemed to work really well for Mark.

The Story has been effective for other children too. Mark never got to like spelling tests but he did in time accept that one or two wrong answers were okay. In time, with additional work on personal best (page 227) he moved on from that concept to eventually accepting much lower scores than 100 per cent in many subsequent tests and exams. Years later in college and during his apprenticeship he even developed the notion of 'close enough', which I truly would never have believed possible in his early school years.

What is a spelling test?

Usually on Monday morning my class has a spelling test. The teacher usually reads out each word and the children write it down.

At the end of the test the teacher collects all the spelling books and marks them.

Sometimes children make mistakes in their spellings. Sometimes grown-ups make mistakes in their spellings too. This is okay. The job of the spelling test is to find out which spellings need more practice.

Staying calm helps my brain remember my spellings. Here are some things I may do to help me stay calm in my spelling test:

Let my shoulders go loose

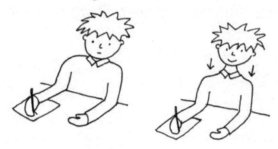

Count to ten penguins

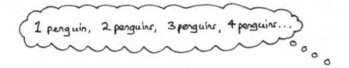

1 penguin, 2 penguins, 3 penguins, 4 penguins...

Feel my hanky in my pocket

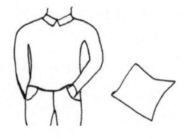

I am learning to stay calm in spelling tests.

Stories about teachers
What does my teacher know?
Why do teachers ask students questions?

Children with autism may not necessarily be aware of a teacher's knowledge – something that naturally leads the neurotypical child to accept information, guidance and even discipline from the teacher. Having a lack of theory of mind may also lead a child with autism to misread the intention behind a teacher's actions, such as the reason why a teacher may be asking students questions in the classroom.

In the first year of college, the course tutor told me that Mark was frequently exasperated when he wasn't chosen to answer a question. Having gathered further details from the tutor and the LSA, I explored this with him in a Comic Strip Conversation (page 34) at home. It became apparent that Mark's perspective was different from mine. He did not understand why if the tutor wanted to know the answer to a question he would choose a student to answer who invariably got the answers wrong, when he had his hand raised and always had the right answers. Mark was highly competent in the subject of IT so this both confused and frustrated him.

This showed me that he was missing some important social information and therefore misunderstood why sometimes teachers ask students questions. He assumed the teacher was asking questions in order to find out the answers because he did not know the answer himself. This is probably what he had been told in the past was the purpose of asking a question. In this particular teacher–student context, however, this was not the reason questions were being asked. The teacher knew the answer but was trying to find out what *the students* knew. When I suggested this as an alternative perspective Mark looked very interested. Many young people with autism struggle with this misunderstanding, and unfortunately many neurotypicals judge their frustrated response negatively as a result.

The previous Story 'My teacher grew up too' outlined the teacher's experience in life as they grew up. The next Story 'What does my teacher know' specifically focused on the teacher's academic learning and teaching experience. This is information may not be apparent to a child or young person with autism, again because they may not be mindful of the teacher's training or expertise because of poor theory of mind. Once this information about the teacher's experience is shared it then makes more sense for children to listen to the teacher and ask him for help, both with the academic subject that is being taught and with questions about growing up.

Another Story 'Why do teachers ask questions?' followed, which shared the perspective of the teacher – that the purpose of his questions was not to find out the answers, which he already knew, but to discover what the students knew. It explained how this information helped the teacher work out the level of understanding across the class, and how to improve the learning of the class. After reading it for the first time Mark smiled and said 'got it!'

Although he still always wanted to be chosen to answer in class, he now understood why he was not always chosen and was no longer upset.

The Stories 'I am still growing up' and 'My teacher grew up too' (page 44), followed later by 'What does my teacher know?' and finally 'Why do teachers ask questions?' build understanding of the student–teacher relationship and set the foundation of classroom life.

What does my teacher know?

My teacher was born many years before I was born and has learned many things. My teacher has been a baby, a child, a teenager, a young man, and now is an adult.

At school his favourite lesson was geography. When my teacher finished school he went to college. At college he studied geography in more detail and passed exams in geography and other subjects.

When my teacher finished college he went to university for three years. His teachers were called lecturers at university. At university the lecturers taught my teacher geography in even more detail.

At the end of university he was awarded a degree in geography, which means my teacher knows and understands geography at a very high level.

After university my teacher went to teacher training college for another year. There he learned how to teach children and qualified as a teacher with a specialist interest in geography.

After teacher training college he taught children geography in schools for many years.

My teacher has spent many years teaching children and young adults. Because he has had all this training and experience he knows a huge amount about geography. This means he is an important person to ask when I need help with understanding geography.

My teacher has also been a baby, a child, a teenager and a young man and he is now an adult. He knows about growing up. For this reason he may be able also to help me understand about growing up.

Sometimes I may have questions about geography and sometimes I may have questions about growing up. My teacher will be pleased to help me.

Why do teachers ask children questions?

Sometimes during a lesson the teacher may ask a question. The teacher usually knows the answer. She wants to find out if the children in the class know the answer. This helps her to improve the lesson so that everyone learns.

Several children may raise their hands. Each child with a raised hand usually has an answer to the question. It may be a correct answer or an incorrect answer.

The teacher chooses who answers the question. She wants to find out what the children know or have learned. Sometimes she chooses a child who has the correct answer.

Sometimes she chooses a child who has an incorrect answer. This is okay. The teacher is finding out what children in the class know and what they have learned in the lesson so far.

When a teacher asks a question and I think I have the correct answer I will try to raise my hand.

Sometimes I will be chosen to answer, sometimes another child will be chosen. This is okay. When another child is chosen, I may write down my answer and show the teacher or my LSA at the end of the lesson.

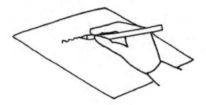

I am learning about why teachers ask children questions in class.

What is the role of the LSA in secondary school?

In secondary school the role of an LSA support may change quite dramatically from that in primary school but frequently there is little explanation given to the child, who may not even know until the day they start the new year who their LSA will be. Sometimes a child may be told that their LSA at a senior school will be 'floating' – a disturbing idea for a literal child!

In secondary school, students may become upset at being assigned an LSA and feel it makes them stand out as different. This was never Mark's experience, as Helen was highly skilled at allowing him to be independent when he was comfortable to do so. As she moved around the classroom and helped other students at their request this actually made her help with Mark seem more part of the general classroom routine.

However, I have been asked several times by schools about students who appeared disrespectful when their LSA asked if they needed help. On gathering information it became clear to me that the students were unaware that their own behaviour was the stimulus for the question and that the LSA was responding according to her training. To understand this a student needs to have a theory of mind allowing him to be mindful of the physical perspective of the LSA, i.e. what she can see from where she is in the classroom, and also what she may surmise from what she sees, i.e. the student is moving around and is therefore no longer focused on the task. Furthermore, her training and job description require her to refocus the student if possible. Theory of mind may not be operating for this student quickly enough or competently enough to provide him with any or all of this information.

The Social Article that follows here was written for a very able secondary school student to explain the role of his LSA.

What is the role of the LSA in secondary school and college?

The learning support assistant (LSA) is a trained member of staff who is a source of support to one or more students in the classroom.

At primary school level he or she is usually allocated to one or two children who need one-to-one help with the lesson. At primary school the LSA usually sits beside the students and helps them throughout the lesson.

At secondary school the LSA is usually available for
all the students as well as their allocated students.
The LSA moves around the class to any student who
requests help. This is called having a 'floating' role within
the classroom. This is how learning support is usually
managed at senior school level.

The LSA usually checks whether her allocated student
needs help by looking to see what her student is doing.
Usually when students are managing to do the work set
they are looking at their books or screen and are working
quietly. This is described as being focused on their work.
Being focused on work shows the LSA that support is not
required at this time.

Sometimes students talk, look around or move from the desk. Usually these actions indicate to the LSA that the student may be unfocused on the work and may need support to refocus, understand the task set, or have a break.

This is why the LSA asks the student if he needs help. The LSA asks the student because making sure the student has any help required is an important part of her job.

Sometimes a student needs to move or look around in order to focus, and does not need help. When a student does not need help he may respond respectfully with a phrase like 'No thank you.'

I will try to remember that the LSA may think I need help if I appear unfocused on my work. When the LSA asks me if I need help and I do not, I will work on, stating respectfully, 'No thank you, I am okay/have finished my work'.

I am learning about the role of the LSA at secondary school level.

Stories about intentions
What is an intention?
Who is in charge of the classroom?

Sometimes neurotypical students find it amusing to ask a student with autism to do something in class that they know will land that student in trouble. The trusting nature of the student with autism, mistakenly interpreting the intentions of the other student as friendly, complies with the request and subsequently is disciplined. This may happen repetitively because the student is so delighted to have another student apparently interacting in a friendly way, and therefore endures the discipline for the 'friendship'. This is such a heartbreaking situation. The student with autism needs missing social information about the intentions of others, and in sharing this with him, his perception of having a friend is shattered, which may be very painful. It needs to be approached sensitively and carefully. Initial work on intentions is a good place to start, and exploration with a Comic Strip Conversation is a great way to do this (Gray, 1994). Sometimes this leads the student to that new understanding and then he may need help to think of other students in the class who have friendly intentions. It may be necessary to facilitate contact with a reliable 'buddy' from the peer group to help the student through this tough realisation.

Comic Strip Conversation is an important part of the gathering of information prior to writing a Social Story™ (page 34). The use of colour in Comic Strip Conversations, to define the underlying intention of the student making the request, is a concrete, visual and extremely useful way to help some students with autism. This technique allows the student to use colour to identify emotions and intentions, and subsequently to try to identify people who have friendly intentions as those people whose colour thoughts match the colour of their words, for example green word people, where green has been identified as a friendly colour. For some children, however, using thought and speech bubbles is confusing and a Comic Strip Conversation cannot be used.

Mark has experienced challenging situations involving the unfriendly intention and motivation of others on several occasions and I have worked with him on questioning people's intentions over many years. It is a work in progress, as his innate trust of other people always hampers his suspicion of their intentions, and his different theory of mind plays a huge part in this. This means that repetition and consistency in the Social Stories™ I write, and how we explore other people's intentions together through CSC is essential, in order to build a 'second nature' thought process over time that will flag up the question 'intention?' in his mind when these situations occur. Because this will be a conscious cognitive process it will, however, always be slower than the innate neurotypical process.

Sometimes the unusual response of the student with autism focuses all the social teaching on him, but it is important to consider that the person who needs help with social understanding here is not just the student with autism, but also the student who is doing the bullying. This needs exploration and addressing too!

I have had several requests for help around similar scenarios concerning the unfriendly intentions of other students. I frequently use the social information and Story format that was successful for Mark, always carefully gathering information first, to address the unique needs of that student.

In more than one scenario a student was being told to perform a song in the middle of class by another student. The student with autism was particularly good at singing and imitating exactly the accent and body movement that accompanied a particular song from a Disney film. However, other students would usually laugh because of the inappropriateness of this recital and the student with autism would be disciplined. Exploration with a Comic Strip Conversation revealed that the student with autism believed that the students loved his song and were his friends because they asked him to sing, interpreting their laughter as a friendly response. He perceived the intention as friendly even though he repetitively got disciplined for disrupting the lesson. Following exploration with a Comic Strip Conversation, which shared the unfriendly intention behind the request, the student needed guidance as to who genuinely appreciated his singing and where it was okay to sing. Work then needed to be put in place to help him work out which students in his class were students with *friendly* intentions behind their friendly words.

Another student was triggered into a predictably angry outburst by the use of a single word, which his unkind peers used to taunt him. Unfortunately, this happened not only repetitively in the classroom, but also during online gaming at home. He had been a successful gamer before and he was now repetitively losing games as a result. The young person was distraught as his home gaming was an outlet and interest for him to recover from the day. It was a dreadful intrusion into the one place he felt secure and content, his home. With his different theory of mind he was unaware of the power of his own response to stop the behaviour of the other child. In sharing with him social information about what the other students were thinking and their intention to make him unsettled, he was empowered to try to control his response, bringing the behaviour of the other children to an end. In this particular scenario a lot of work had previously been done in trying to get the child to control his angry response from the perspective that if he calmed down he would not get into trouble. The work with a Comic Strip Conversation gave him time to visualize in a concrete way the *intention* of the other students and this gave him a logical reason to calm his response.

Young people with autism who have experienced unfriendly behaviour from many others in different situations throughout their life may understandably develop a strong paranoia built on their bad experience. They may perceive unfriendly intention and motivation in nearly every interaction, even when it is not there. So sometimes their attention needs to be drawn to the *friendly* intentions of others and the subsequent interactions that occur. Frequently refocusing the student on this may go some way to redress the balance.

The following Social Stories™ and Articles were written for the two different secondary school students. The first was written for the student who was being provoked deliberately in class. The final illustrations summarising a series of Comic Strip Conversation are included within the text. The text within the thought and speech bubbles matched the colour chosen by the student to portray 'friendly' and 'unfriendly' ideas or emotions. This is an example of how the work done in a CSC may lead into a Social Story™. The illustrations used highlight the key points of the Story. For the visual thinker, recall of these pictures may be easier than recall of the Story content. I have used my own drawings here in the genre that was meaningful for Mark.

The second Story was for the student who needed a general rule to guide him on his response to others' requests in the classroom, allowing him to take time away from the situation to explore the intention of other students with his learning support assistant. He also needed time to process which requests were friendly requests so that he could respond in a friendly manner.

In all these kinds of bullying situations it is important always to emphasise to a child that he has a team around him who can help and that they want to do so. Then the team need to actively support him!

What is an intention?

An intention is the reason a person says or does something. An intention may be friendly or unfriendly. Usually when a person says friendly words they have friendly reasons for saying the words. They have friendly intentions.

Sometimes a person may say friendly words but at the same time have unfriendly reasons for saying these words. They have unfriendly intentions.

In my school there are many students who have friendly intentions and only a few students who have unfriendly intentions. Sometimes it is easy to work out intentions, sometimes it is tricky.

When a student says or does something that unsettles me I may think about whether their intention is friendly or unfriendly. If I think their intention is unfriendly I will try to stay calm. Staying calm helps my brain think. Sometimes staying calm stops the student trying to unsettle me.

To help me stay calm I may choose one of my calming strategies.

If I am unsure about a student's intention I may write down what the student said and ask Mrs M after the lesson. Mrs M knows about friendly and unfriendly intentions. She will help me decide.

I am learning about intentions.

Who is in charge of the classroom?

At school the teacher is usually in charge of the classroom. This means that the teacher gives the instructions to the students. Occasionally the LSA will be in charge while the teacher is out of the class. Usually the students try to follow the teacher or the LSA's instructions.

Sometimes a student tells another student to do something in the class. Sometimes the student is being friendly and sometimes the student is being unfriendly. This may be difficult to work out sometimes. I will try to remember it is the teacher's job or the LSA's job to give students instructions in class.

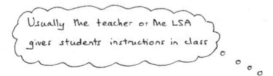

Usually the teacher or the LSA gives students instructions in class

When another student gives me an instruction in class I may ignore them and write down what I was asked to do. After the lesson Mrs B will help me decide whether the student's intention was friendly or unfriendly.

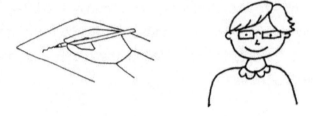

The teacher and Mrs B will be pleased with me.

Stories about handwriting
I am learning handwriting
What is the reason for learning handwriting?

'Practice makes perfect' is a phrase often used by teachers and parents to encourage children to practise handwriting. Neurotypical children innately develop an underlying understanding of the concept of practice from frequent self-reflection on times in the past when they have practised a new skill and become better at it, even without achieving perfection. So when neurotypical children hear that phrase, they understand that in this context the teacher is not actually expecting immediate perfection. Of course, neurotypical children still become frustrated when practice does not deliver quick improvement, but they are usually easily reassured by reference to previous successful experience.

In the classroom, a teacher may direct children to copy the writing from a printed poster by saying, 'I want you to copy it down just like it's written here on this poster'. The neurotypical child understands that she means *as close as possible* to the printed writing – he understands the underlying meaning of her words in this context. The child with autism, however, may follow her instruction a-contextually and therefore literally. He may try to make his letters exactly like the printed type and, of course, fail to do so and become very frustrated. Using accurate literal instruction is essential when introducing handwriting for the first time and particularly when directing children with autism to copy from print. Describing expectation of their likely attempt is important here. This helps them have realistic expectations of themselves and the handwriting they produce. In fact, the introduction of any new skill or concept in school should be done using literal and accurate language if there is a child with autism in the class. However, I am fairly sure that there are very few lesson plans that describe why we need to do handwriting in this day and age and what the difference is between printed and handwritten letters.

It may help to have concrete visual examples of the development of handwriting over time to show children how everyone's handwriting starts off and eventually ends up. I used my early school exercise books to demonstrate to Mark how my writing developed, having removed any specific timeframe reference so as not to add any pressure. This could easily be done from other children's practice examples, always being careful not to compare someone else's progress in a way that flattens self-esteem.

Children with autism frequently struggle with handwriting for various reasons. This means that gathering information for the individual child is critical to avoid the pitfall of making an assumption about the cause of the difficulty according to our own neurotypical perspective. Some children may be struggling to make their writing 'just like' the printed writing because of their literal understanding of the teacher's instruction. Some children may be struggling with the idea of making a mistake. Some may not understand that handwriting is unique to each individual and is meant to be so. Others may not realise that printed writing is made by a machine and therefore each letter is always the same and perfect and that this is not possible to do by hand.

Physical difficulties with fine motor control and co-ordination may also hamper a child's progress too, so there needs to be careful exploration of the individual child's perspective, his physical ability and the situation before a Story topic is identified. This is important because any one or all of these difficulties can eventually lead a child to refuse to try to write, and because writing is still an important part of most lessons at primary school this may lead to a disengagement with the whole learning process.

As handwriting is such a common worry among our children and I am so frequently asked if a Social Story™ can help, I have included two successful Stories here that were written for children who required different levels of support.

The Stories were not written specifically for Mark, but they contain important elements of the social information I shared with him around handwriting which helped him continue to learn and practise.

The first Story was written for a child with autism who was intolerant of his handwriting not being perfect like print, a very common scenario. The Social Story 'What is practice?' (page 86) was individualised for him and refreshed first because an understanding of the concept of practice is necessary before working on handwriting.

The second Story was written as a Social Article for an older, higher functioning child, who did not see the point of learning to write at all in the digital age and refused to do so. He already had dispensation to use a laptop for exams. Following the Story he, begrudgingly, agreed to do some practice as it now made slightly more sense to him! Surprisingly up until that point the argument for learning to write by hand had been made with reference to exams and classwork notes only.

Within this second Story is the word 'unique'. This student had clear understanding of the meaning of the word unique, so it is not defined within the Story. This is a very important and useful word to understand if you have an ASC, so I would recommend that all students are taught its meaning and that their understanding of it is checked.

Before introducing these Stories I asked the parents to highlight to their child times when they used handwriting in real life, just as I had done for Mark, for example on cheques, shopping lists, writing a birthday card, addressing an envelope or just leaving a note for each other. Trying to read a message left by another adult is an ideal opportunity to highlight the importance of others being able to read what we write, which gives a logical reason to practise handwriting at school. After all, we are unlikely to leave our laptop behind with a message on it when we go out to the local supermarket – we leave a handwritten note. Sometimes we need to stick a handwritten note on the fridge door or a broken lift door so that everyone can see it and understand the message. Text messaging everyone who may walk past is impossible! It helps to use an example of a written message that contains information which the child clearly sees as important to him, for example in Mark's case, 'Don't forget to buy more Jaffa Cakes!' was very meaningful.

I also asked parents to emphasise the particular importance of signatures on cheques, agreements and contracts, as a way of identifying the person exactly *because* they don't look like printing and are unique to the individual.

There is a lot of scope for practically supporting these Stories. An example might be a survey by the child of the handwriting or signatures of all the children in the class, which concretely demonstrates that difference is the norm. Another example could be identifying signatures on important historical documents in history by famous people. This would really engage students with a special interest in history!

All the work done around addressing handwriting issues is in fact an opportunity to begin the concept of identity which becomes more important as time goes by – the idea that we are all unique and this is the most wonderful thing about human beings and should be celebrated.

I am learning handwriting

At school I am learning handwriting.
Handwriting comes from holding a pen or pencil
and moving it along a piece of paper to make
letters and words.

When children start to learn their handwriting
is usually wobbly.

The dog

The dog

The dog

The dog

With practice, children's fingers learn what to
do and the writing gets less wobbly. This makes
the letters and words easier to read.

When handwriting is easy to read other people can understand what it means. This is the reason we practise handwriting at school.

Sometimes children copy printed writing when they are practising handwriting.

 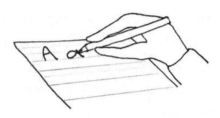

Printed writing comes from a machine like a computer or laptop. Each letter is neat and always the same because it is made by a machine. This makes it easy to read.

Handwriting usually looks different to printed writing. This is okay. Handwriting is meant to look different to printed writing.

Sometimes when I do my handwriting it looks different to printed writing. This is okay. With practice my handwriting is getting closer to handwriting that is easy to read.

I am learning handwriting.

What is the reason for learning handwriting?

Nowadays many people use laptops and computers to write, but there are still times when people use handwriting. Sometimes people need to write a message quickly to tell another person something. They may need to put the message on a piece of paper and place it where another person may see it. This may be done by handwriting. The message may contain important information. An example may be 'Lift broken, use stairs' or 'Turn oven off at 2pm' or 'Gran is sick, have gone to see her'. Being able to write clearly is useful so that others can read the message.

Sometimes on a special occasion people write a message in a birthday card or congratulations card. Being able to write clearly is helpful here too, so others can read the message.

Sometimes people write their own name in handwriting as a signature. Everyone's handwriting is different and everyone's signature is different. A signature is therefore an important way of identifying a person because each person's signature is unique to that person, like a fingerprint.

Mum writes her signature on a cheque so the bank knows she has approved the cheque to be paid. Dad and Mum put their signatures on a contract to hire a car on holiday. Their signatures were proof that they had agreed the contract. I signed my learner agreement at college. My signature was proof that I agreed to the agreement.

Sometimes machines stop working. Sometimes phones are unable to receive text messages. When this happens a person may need to write things down by hand instead of printing them.

Some students learn to write clearly quickly; some students take longer. This is okay. Nowadays a lot of writing is done by using machines and this helps students who take longer to learn handwriting. Still, with practice, writing by hand gets closer to writing that is easy to read.

For all these important reasons students learn to write by hand at school and practise to make their handwriting easy to read.

Stories about homework
What is homework?
How to make homework more comfy

The word 'homework' universally instils dread into the hearts and minds of children with autism and their parents. Homework had the same effect on my son and myself and I have met many many parents who report finding homework one of the most distressing pressures on their family lives during the school and college years. To understand why it caused such distress in our children I recently asked my son again who told me emphatically and without any hesitation 'because home is home and school is school'. I am just beginning to develop some understanding of this perspective.

The word homework is the combination of two words from two completely opposite worlds, 'home' and 'work'. 'Home', my son's favourite word, evokes a sanctuary of comfort and understanding: a place, in fact the only place, where he can feel happy to be himself, pursue his own interests and be totally loved and accepted. It is the place where he recuperates at the end of the day, rebuilding himself ready for the next day's challenges: a place of blissful solitude and recovery on his terms.

'Work' is devised and carried out at school, away from home. School is frequently experienced as an uncomfortable sensory environment with hugely challenging social situations for the child with autism. In this environment, 'work' may be difficult and presented in language that may be inaccessible.

To the logical mind 'work' therefore belongs in the 'work place' and 'home' belongs at home. They absolutely should not be in the same place in a word together, never mind being in the same place together.

The purpose of setting homework is twofold. First, there is consolidation of work covered during school hours or preparation work for the subject being taught in the following days. Second, there is preparation of the child or student for independent study outside the work place. This is an uncomfortable task initially, until a student becomes accustomed to it. It requires practice, initially starting on small amounts of work, such as reading with a parent for a young child, building up to long periods of independent study for a sixth former or university student. The self-discipline of independent study is a learned skill. And it is not just for those who choose an academic path. Nowadays apprenticeships require their students to be self-motivated learners, keeping to assignment deadlines and completing much of this work at home. Once within the workplace continued professional development means that workers are expected to continue some study from time to time to keep up to date.

There wasn't a lesson on 'the purpose of homework' at my school or any of my sons' schools but there is a need for it. Homework is just presented to children as an important and compulsory part of education. Little time is given to explaining the purpose behind it but a lot of time is spent describing the penalties if it is not completed to a certain standard or handed in by a specific deadline. Parents immediately feel stressed that their child may be deemed less capable than they actually are if they do not produce what is required, and so place pressure on the child to engage with it, and frequently do it themselves to help their child. And so it starts – the world of school enters the world of home, along with all its discomforts and pressures, the one place where our young person should feel pressure free and most comfortable.

There are other reasons children with autism give me for their intense dislike of homework. Some say it is the pressure to do it after a day full of pressures, others say that the frustration that it is never finished is overwhelming – as soon as one lot is completed another lot is set. Unreasonable setting of homework is also a problem, with students being set work instead of it being covered in class, or homework unrelated to classwork being set, just for 'homework's sake.

Homework being used as a disciplinary measure also happens unfortunately.

Using the term 'preparation work' is helpful as it describes the original purpose – where the child or student did work outside of school to prepare for the next lesson and to prepare for independent study. This term would be more meaningful for work done at home once in the workplace too.

Over many years I have found it helpful for Mark to explain a purpose to something that is compulsory, validate his feelings around it and then adapt it as much as is possible to make it more comfortable and feasible. So I wrote the following Social Story™ to explain the purpose of homework and to acknowledge that it was a difficult thing to learn to do. Then, using much of Tony Attwood's excellent advice around homework (Attwood, 2008), I wrote another Story about 'How to make homework more comfy'.

Frequently, students with autism forget to bring the books or materials they need to complete homework at home. It really helped to have a set of spare homework materials at home so that

Mark had all he needed, including pens, pencils, geometry set, ruler, graph paper and also a spare set of textbooks where possible, from the school.

But probably the most helpful thing I did was to negotiate a limit to the time spent on homework and to absolutely stick to this. Beginning at only ten minutes, we gradually built up to an hour over many weeks. Each evening, once the time set was reached, he stopped working and I wrote in the homework diary that he had completed the time. Parents are usually so keen for their child to succeed that they often, even without realising they are doing it, encourage the child to do just a little more, or 'just finish this topic' and the limit can be exceeded, sometimes resulting in the child losing trust in the scheme.

Teachers can also help with a positive and timely response to mark a student's efforts at homework. Work left unmarked for days or even weeks reduces any positive reinforcement of the attempt at the work and makes the whole effort seem unreasonable. Many parents have found that their child sees the work as 'pointless' if no one marks it. However, many children with autism become distressed if homework is returned covered in red pen for correction. Although it is of course necessary to correct mistakes, some acknowledgement of the effort rather than just the outcome is really important in children with autism, for the reasons outlined above.

Mark's LSA, Helen, worked hard to be Mark's advocate in the setting and completion of homework and was extremely effective in putting his case forward, so that between us the demands of homework were made much more manageable. When work was set as assignments or projects where there was a choice of topic, Helen and I would choose subjects from Mark's special interest that would really engage him. Working on these then needed no time limitation because it was enjoyable. A highly successful example of this would be the English speaking assignment where each student had to choose a topic to talk about in a short presentation to the class, which would be marked as an examination. Mark naturally chose penguins and so to help gather information at the weekend we went to the penguin arena at the zoo and took impressions on tracing paper from the life size drawings of the different types of penguins. Mark then made cardboard cut-outs of these at home and painted them. He then chose what he wanted to say about each penguin and wrote it on different pieces of paper which were then stuck on the back of each penguin. He then held the penguin up and read his notes, although he did not really need these as he remembered them very well on the day. The largest penguin, the Emperor penguin, was the same height as he was and it stood beside him like a friend, giving him confidence. Needless to say this worked well.

In order to maximise relaxation time and minimise homework time all through primary school I encouraged the boys to learn their tables in the car on the way to school for 20 minutes out of a 40-minute journey. Every day it was someone's turn to choose the voice that the tables were recited in. The voice could be Piglet's voice, Darth Vader's voice, even a guinea pig squeak voice. This made it fun and by the end of the week the table had been recited for 1 hour and 40 minutes without anyone feeling like they had been doing 'homework' at all, and with no intrusion on home time. The spellings we learned by the 'seeing, saying, writing then checking' technique, folding the piece of paper over after each one. Once the piece of paper was completely folded into a thick strip, homework was over. This was a very effective, concrete and visual way of showing Mark how long it was until homework was finished.

Having a clear understanding of when homework starts and finishes helps to bring predictability, and a visual timetable constructed with the child's cognitive level clearly in mind can really help here. I also recommend the use of a visual timer where the passage of time is clearly visible and the child can see how much time *remains* on task. Mark used my kitchen timer!

The homework problem cannot be solved with just a Social Story™ because the solution comes from teachers and parents understanding the experience of autism for the child, leading to a co-operative effort to adapt what is required to be meaningful and comfortable for an exhausted child with autism. The tiredness a child with autism experiences at the end of a school day is on a completely different level to that of a neurotypical child. Struggling with sensory overload, lack of coherence and a different theory of mind increases the child's anxiety levels. The child is unable to find relief from the fun activities built into the school programme, like break time, which refresh the neurotypical children, because these cause him even more anxiety. We all know how exhausting being highly anxious is, because we have all experienced such anxiety before for a short period, perhaps, for example, in a job interview. For a child with autism, school may mean experiencing that level of anxiety for a full day, every day. Teachers therefore need to be aware of the need to carefully set work with a time limit that is within the child's capability *when tired*. Every opportunity to do homework in free lessons at school should be taken advantage of, and if subjects are dropped closer to public examinations then these free periods should be used in this way to relieve the child of study when he gets home.

Mark was very fortunate, and together with the special needs department, we were able to negotiate a reduced number of GCSE exam subjects for him (six in total), which allowed him some free time at school for study and eliminated subjects that he found difficult because of his autism. Helen always aimed to have most homework covered in the lesson periods that were freed up as a result. This flexibility is now much more commonplace in schools and I believe is the secret of keeping children with autism engaged and learning in mainstream settings.

As Mark passed through the education system and needed to plan what he was going to do after school I was able to show him, in a concrete and visual way, the studying requirements of apprenticeships, which was his preferred route of progression towards a job. Brochures describing courses clearly stated how much study would be required and also how much time needed to be spent in the college. We could then work out together how and when he could complete this work during the day so there was no infringement on his leisure time in the evening. Allowing plenty of recuperation time was very effective in the levels of anxiety being manageable.

The following Stories describe the purpose of homework and how to make homework more 'comfy'. Mark started homework in Year 1 at primary school and so by secondary school was getting used to the concept. Many children first encounter homework at secondary school, and this is usually when I am asked about how to address an issue with a Social Story™. This usually follows a homework refusal. These following Stories/Articles use the information given to Mark at primary level in language and format more suitable to an older or more able child.

I hope they might inspire parents and professionals to build this information into an introduction to homework that will be meaningful for the child with autism, and then practise flexibility in the timetable to consider their needs for free time at home.

What is homework?

Sometimes teachers give students work to do at home. Sometimes this is to check that the student has understood the lesson. Sometimes it is to give the student extra practice on the skills learned in the lesson.

It is called homework because it is done at home rather than in school. Really all homework is preparation work. Some schools call it preparation work or 'prep' for short. It may help me to think of homework as preparation work both for school and for learning away from school.

Children begin to practise how to learn at home when they are very young. Reading with Mum or Dad is a good way to start learning at home. As children grow up and mature they do more of their learning by themselves.

When students finish school they may go on to university or an apprenticeship or into the workplace. In all of these places there will be some study to do at home by themselves.

Spending some time at home learning rather than doing fun things is a skill that needs practice like many other skills. Like many other new skills, it may feel uncomfortable at first but with practice it gets better.

I am learning about homework in secondary school.

How to make homework more comfy

There are a few things that many students have discovered make homework more comfy. I may find they help me too. They are:

1. Making sure I have the right homework details by:

   writing them down in a homework diary

   asking my LSA to write them down for me

having a homework buddy from my class to call.

2. Having a back-up set of homework materials at home.

3. Choosing a place to do my homework that is mine and making it comfy.

4. Getting my homework done early so it is finished and I can relax.

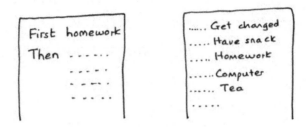

5. Doing my homework only for a specific time agreed with my teacher and using a timer.

6. Asking Mum or Dad if I get stuck.

Sometimes I will get my homework done within the agreed time. Sometimes I will do some but not all of it. This is okay. I have worked at home for the agreed time. Mum will usually sign my work with the time I started and finished.

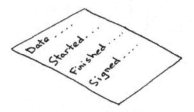

My teacher will see Mum's signature and know that I have worked at my homework for the agreed time.

As I grow older I am learning to get more done in the agreed time. I am learning about homework at secondary school.

What is revision?

Revision is sometimes introduced in late primary school, with usually just a brief description of what it means. Perhaps the teacher might describe it as 'going over what we have done on this topic' or 'looking again at what you have learned about this topic' to 'get ready' for a test. This is, of course, quite enough for neurotypical children to get the gist of what is expected. For the child with autism, however, there may be insufficient information in this description. For this child more literally accessible detail may be needed. He may feel quite sure already of what he knows and has learned. Often he sees no reason to 'look' at learned work again and therefore may object to doing so. 'Look' to a literal child may not carry the same neurotypical meaning of 'learn'. There is therefore a need to define it for everyone in a little more detail early on and then refine the definition more specifically in secondary school. This is helpful for all children in the class, not just for those with autism. For those things in life that are unavoidable, having meaningful understanding of the purpose often brings tolerance.

In primary school revision of topics may mean the simple regurgitation of facts, which many children with autism can do well, and sometimes exceptionally well. However, at secondary school the interpretation of facts from a different perspective is often needed and simple recall is not enough to score highly in tests and exams. To the child who has always been confident of their recall and performance this can come as quite a shock, and therefore these children may require exploration of their knowledge with practice questions in revision sessions to accustom them to the type of question there may be in the test or exam, and also to shape their information to fit the answer correctly. Work around the intention of the examiner in his question is important as a literal interpretation of the question, along with a lack of insight into the intention behind the question, may lead to wrong answers and low scores.

Mark has always had a great memory and did have excellent recall of facts covered in the classroom. However, moulding his answers to fit the question was more tricky. We worked hard to analyse common question stems with him, looking for 'action' words and clues as to the intention behind the question, often supporting this with a comic strip featuring the examiner with a thought bubble, and linking that to appropriate answers. Using colour to link the action word to the required response was helpful too.

Some examination boards, even at a higher level, may introduce a question with a story, the detail of which may completely confuse the student with autism. This may be done with the intention of engaging the child with, for example, the context of a mathematics problem. However, the child with autism will often stall on a name he has not met before, or be confused by the description of a real-life situation he has not encountered, and therefore without good social imagination, he cannot understand the question. For a bright child with lots of information to share this may be very frustrating.

During Mark's time in further education, tackling the compulsory functional mathematics attached to his chosen subject of business administration, we spent time ensuring he understood what the many different common construction parts of a house were, for example skirting boards, by pointing these out around the house and in the local DIY store. This built his visual understanding of the vocabulary that might typically surface in his exam, affecting his ability to understand the question.

Mark has experienced many frustrations with exam and test questions throughout his education. He was also always reluctant to revise. I wrote the following Social Article for him in secondary school purely to explain 'revision' after he told me he knew what he knew, and had no reason to look for it because he knew where and what it was. Following the Social Article he agreed to read his work through and did some practice questions. He was very surprised to discover that he did in fact have a few areas that needed further understanding. Having a better understanding of the purpose of revision helped him accept it more readily, although he was never enthusiastic about it! I guess very few neurotypicals enjoy revision either so *this is okay*!

What is revision?

To do revision usually means to refresh knowledge. Teachers often ask students to revise topics in order to prepare for exams. The purpose of revision for exams is to refresh what students already know and to strengthen the bits of knowledge that may need more understanding or learning. Doing revision usually helps improve the final score in an exam.

One way of finding the bits that need more learning is to answer practice questions. Many students think it is smart to find out what they know using practice questions to check their scores.

Sometimes students remember all they have learned well and score highly in practice questions. Occasionally students discover topics they need to understand better, learn more thoroughly or have more teaching on.

Sometimes reading topics again makes knowledge stronger. Sometimes a teacher can help with topics that need more understanding. Some students make short notes or use illustrations to help remember a topic. Each student usually finds a method of revision that works best for him or her.

Teachers usually know several different methods of revision. They can help find the method that works best for each student.

My best method of revision is...

Doing revision may help improve my final score in an exam.

Going Home

Viv is picking me up today

I usually picked Mark and his brothers up from primary school. Very occasionally I would be unable to do so and would ask a good friend to drop him home. However, Mark would feel extremely unsettled if there was a change to his routine. Our journey home together from school was an important part of his day when he transitioned back to the comfort of his sanctuary, home. The car, with his Mum beside him, was a mobile extension of his home! If this routine was in any way different he would become very anxious. The anxiety and distress around changes are difficult to eliminate completely but I frequently noted that more information around the context of the changing situation definitely diminished his anxiety. Social Stories™ are extremely effective in relieving anxiety about what is going to happen when a routine is changed.

A Social Story™ would not stand alone in preparation for this event. I would plan ahead and ask someone he knew well to bring him home. I would ensure they knew all about him and understood how to help him manage. Because of his different theory of mind, Mark was unable to be mindful of what the person who was bringing him home might know about him. Sometimes I would demonstrate in a concrete way to him that I had written down this information for the person. Mark also needed this information written down for him in a Social Story so that he could take time to read it, think about it and understand it. First, I explored his perspective with him in a drawing conversation to discover which things were of paramount importance for his babysitter to know. I had identified most of them myself but was frequently surprised by a detail that I had not considered. These details might change from time to time. Spending time to gather information is always beneficial even when the author feels confident of the information required, and it is often the fine detail that is critically important to the child. This very simple straightforward Story was of huge benefit in allaying Mark's anxiety.

A Social Story™ like this can make a huge difference to the child's whole day. Being anxious about how you are going to get home escalates easily into distress over the course of a school day and can be so simply avoided by sharing the information with the child. It may not of course remove all anxiety; there is still going to be anxiety around the change taking place but knowing when the new situation will begin and end, and who is going to be there and what they know brings clarity to confusion and comfort to distress.

Sometimes parents and professionals are reluctant to mention an imminent change to a child with autism before it happens, because of the depth of upset caused by it, hoping to get through the inevitable distress as quickly as possible. Initially when he was very young I would sometimes do the 'scoop and run' approach to getting Mark into his car seat, simply to reduce the length of time he was upset for. But when I learned about visual timetables and Social Stories™ I found that as he learned to trust the message a Social Story brought, he was reassured and surprisingly comfortable after reading it. Over the years I have noted that, in many cases, our children are actually more flexible to change than we sometimes anticipate – it is the information and predictability that they are missing and which causes the massive anxiety. So here is an example of an early, very simple, successful Social Story entitled 'Who is picking me up today?'

This very simple Story format was used again when I was away from home overnight in 'Mum and Dad are going to a meeting' (page 158).

Viv is picking me up today

My school usually finishes at about three o'clock. My Mum usually takes me home when school finishes.

Sometimes Mum asks someone else to take me home. Mum will usually tell me who is taking me home. This is okay.

Today Mum has asked Viv to take me home.

Mum has told Viv about what happens at home. Viv knows what to do. Viv knows what I like for tea. This is okay.

Mum is coming home after tea. Mum will be pleased to see me.

Viv is picking me up from school today.

Mum and Dad are going to a meeting

Children with autism may be unable, or less able, to identify and make sense of the clues that are socially relevant to the situation they find themselves in. When something changes in their environment they are less able to predict what might happen next and therefore feel unprepared and highly anxious. They are missing important reassuring social information, information we neurotypicals take for granted. Therefore, when the regular rhythm of life at home is disrupted it may be extremely alarming and distressing for them. Sharing the social information they are missing in an accessible and logical way with a Social Story™ may bring great comfort.

Very occasionally I was away from home overnight during the school term and when this happened (usually to attend an autism conference), Mark would become highly anxious. This anxiety was allayed to some extent by keeping to his usual routines and having a very familiar family member taking my role. What really helped though was describing in a Social Story what the situation was, when it would most likely start and finish, and what the key people involved knew about him and his needs, so they could help him feel okay.

This is a very important role for Social Stories™ – to prepare a child for a change by providing this missing information. As authors we can try to predict what information the child may need by reflecting on his different perspective. Once a Story is written its effectiveness should be carefully monitored and if extra information is required after the event it can be added in. The next time a similar situation arises the Story can be read again and its similarity can be highlighted to the child along with praise about how he managed the situation before. In this way we are not just preparing him for future changes but also gathering information and acting as a 'context store', helping the child to identify similar contexts and self-reflect on past successful social achievements. We are building bit by bit some resilience to change.

On one memorable occasion I took my husband to a two-day conference to learn about writing Social Stories™. This was the first time we had stayed away from Mark so we were all anxious!

I was extremely fortunate to have two people who understood Mark, were receptive to my directions and were knowledgeable about his autism – Viv and Helen. One of them would usually be available to stay over at home to keep the routines and allow Mark to feel comfortable. However, this kind support needed a Social Story™ at its heart. The Story needed in particular to explain what Viv or Helen would know about Mark and his important routines, as Mark was not mindful of this because of his different social understanding. As a result of the Story, although Mark would always prefer me not to go, he understood that I would return and that the people caring for him knew what to do. He was reassured.

There were other strategies that I put in place to help him feel more comfortable in my absence. Mindful of his acute sense of smell I would spray a very small amount of my perfume near his pillow and sometimes would give him my own pillowcase so that my scent would be nearby. I recorded a message telling him how much I loved him and that I would be back soon onto a small heart recorder that was placed inside a teddy bear that he had made at Build-A-Bear-Workshop™.

When anxious in the night he could press the bear's tummy to hear my voice and could smell my scent close to him on his pillow. These little steps, combined with the maintenance of his usual routine, and this Social Story™, really helped.

Mum and Dad are going to a meeting

Mrs M and Mrs B usually look after me at school.

Mum and Dad usually look after me at home.

Sometimes Mum and Dad go to a meeting.
Mum and Dad are going to a meeting today.

The meeting is a long way to travel so they will stay in a hotel for one night's sleep and come home tomorrow. This is okay.

Mrs B will take me home today when school is finished. Mum has told Mrs B about what happens at home. Mrs B knows what to do. Mrs B will look after me at home today.

Mrs B knows what I like for tea.

Mrs B knows what bubbles to put in my bath.

Mrs B knows my favourite bedtime story is...
She knows that the light stays on in my room.

Mrs B will help me get dressed and have
breakfast in the morning. She knows that I like
my cereal without milk.

Mrs B will take me to school in the morning and will take me home tomorrow when school finishes.

Mum and Dad will be home after tea. Mum and Dad will be pleased to see me.

Break Time

What happens at break time?

Break time at school, whether at primary or secondary level, has a distinct purpose. Children who have been sitting still for a couple of hours concentrating hard on school work are allowed to let off steam, releasing their pent up energy, and are encouraged to engage in enjoyable activities in order to refresh themselves and get ready for further lessons.

Everyone has a different way of calming down and everyone has a different way of refreshing themselves and relaxing. What works for one child or adult may not work for another and what works for a neurotypical child may not work for a child with autism.

Because neurotypicals are very focused on 'social' behaviour we may easily make the mistake of insisting that the child with autism is engaged socially with other children at break time. We see this as 'having fun' because social behaviour is relaxing and fun for us. It may not be relaxing and fun for the child with autism; in fact it is quite often quite the opposite. Our children go out to break time already exhausted by the effort of coping with the sensory, social and language challenges of the morning. Unsuccessful social interactions in the playground result in rejection and confusion, compounding their feelings of frustration and failure. The noise of a large group of children playing may be uncomfortable or even painful. They may return to the classroom, not in a refreshed state ready to begin study, but in absolute distress. Sometimes this is augmented by the next activity or lesson on the timetable being one that is inaccessible for them.

I feel very strongly that break time should be a source of relaxation for a child with autism just as it is for a neurotypical child. This is only fair. The child with autism is under much greater stress than the majority of his classmates. So finding ways to relax in the way that already works for him is essential. Allowing the child to be alone in a quiet area is absolutely okay. The area should be established as a safe place to go, and will quickly be seen as a refuge from the chaos of the playground. Many schools suggest the special needs room, a quiet room or a library where a member of staff can oversee the children there. Clubs that connect children with similar interests may refresh the child and build social relationships. However, if the child needs to pace the perimeter fence alone to unwind and recover he should be allowed to do so.

I have been asked to write Stories to encourage children with autism to join in games and make friends in the playground on many occasions. I wrote the following Story for Mark to describe the purpose of break time and what the different options were for him. I felt it was very important to add within the Story that if he wanted to be alone then that was okay too. It has always been my objective to respectfully share social information with Mark so that he had the ability to join a social group when he wanted or needed to, but I have never enforced it or demanded it of him.

What happens at break time?

At school children usually work hard in lessons. At break time children usually stop work and relax. Break time mostly happens outside in the playground. Sometimes when it is raining break time happens indoors in the hall.

Relaxing at break time usually helps children get ready for the next lessons. Some children like to run to relax. This is okay.

Some children like to play a game to relax. This is okay.

Some children like to talk to other children to relax. This is okay.

Some children like to be on their own in a quiet place to relax. This is okay too.

At break time:

I may join a game or

I may talk to another child or

I may run around or

I may be on my own in a quiet place or
maybe do something else.

Usually the junior library is a quiet place to go
at break time. Relaxing at break time usually
helps me get ready for the next lessons.

I am learning what happens at break time.

Who is the owner of a game in the playground?

The most confident and popular children in the playground are the most likely to initiate a game and recruit others to join them. They are sometimes given temporary 'ownership' of the game they have begun by the other children involved, and with that comes the authority to change the rules as they wish, and also to allow other children to join the game, or refuse to let them. Without an understanding of who 'owns' the game the child with autism may valiantly cling on to the order that rules bring, and will fight his corner insisting that the rules absolutely cannot be changed, losing friends along the way.

Before difficulties and conflicts arise in the playground it makes sense to describe these unwritten, unspoken rules so that the child with autism is equipped with the same information as his peers. A Social Story™ describing 'Who owns a game in the playground' was therefore written to explain what the 'owner' of the game was and how sometimes the owner of a game temporarily changes the rules of the game. Changing rules will never be comfortable for the child with autism in the playground but with better understanding comes less frustration and greater tolerance over time.

Games that have set rules which are less likely to be changed are far easier to learn and understand and Mark quickly learned that football was usually played to the same set of rules each time, and that the 'captain' of the team was much more easily identified. By the time Mark finished school he was a fearless and able goalie. The rules around the goalie's role in football are fairly straightforward, and each lunchtime Mark would be happy in goal being part of a team and weathering the banter as best he could. Football banter between players was another area that needed exploration with a Comic Strip Conversation and Social Stories™! Playing in any other position apart from goal was always difficult because it required him to consider what the other players were thinking, something he could do given time, but not quickly enough to be successful in the game.

In recent years I have heard children use the verb to 'own' in a completely different way. 'I totally owned that game' might now mean that 'I was very skilled at it and won easily'. This may cause confusion for those with autism who may be unable to read the context, and therefore misunderstand the intended meaning. I would advise authors to do some research on current playground language before writing Stories for this social minefield.

Who is the owner of a game in the playground?

Sometimes at break time children play in the playground. Sometimes a child begins a new game. The child usually asks other children to join in. He may use friendly words like 'Who wants to play...?'

Usually if others want to play then a game begins. Sometimes the child who began the game is called the 'owner' of the game.

The owner of the game usually decides how the game is played. Sometimes the owner of the game may alter the rules of the game just for this game. This is okay.

When the game is played at another time the rules may return to normal.

The owner of the game usually decides who can join the game and who cannot join the game. When the game is finished the owner is no longer the owner of the game.

Sometimes I may like playing the game. Other times I may dislike the game and want to stop. This is okay. I may play another game or be on my own. This is okay too.

I am learning about games in the playground.

How to join a game in the playground

Mark enjoyed his own company in the playground but occasionally he wanted to join in the games others were playing too. He loved the early games of chasing which were relatively easy to understand, and he was good at these because he was a fast and tireless runner. Over time the games became more complex with more rules and sometimes it became difficult for Mark to work out what was going on, and join in.

Joining a game is not just a single straightforward question; it involves quite sophisticated social skills and it is no surprise that children with autism find this task very difficult. Having observed that Mark clearly wanted at times to engage and join in but was being unsuccessful at doing so, I needed to share some social information with him. Having established in a previous Story the purpose of break time and that it is okay to play alone or with others, I decided to describe an effective way to join a game on a simple level should he want to do so. The following Story describes a simple compliment about a game followed by a simple request to join.

Mark also needed to be prepared for the answer to his request. Mostly this answer would be yes, but occasionally it was no. Rejection for anyone is uncomfortable, so gentle guidance on what to do if the owner of the game says no was added.

When this Story was first reviewed and put in place, I asked a kind classmate who was very caring towards Mark to step in when there was a rejection and play another game with him, or just walk along beside him. As she liked Mark she was happy to help. The Story was read each evening for several days. At the end of a week it was reported that Mark was sometimes walking the perimeter fence alone and sometimes asking to join a game and being successfully included.

How to join a game in the playground

Sometimes at break time children play games together. Sometimes I watch the children playing.

Sometimes I want to be on my own. This is okay. Sometimes I want to join in the game. This is okay too.

Moving closer to the game and using friendly words usually helps me to join a game.

Other children usually like friendly words. Some friendly words to use may be 'Cool game' and 'Can I join in?' or 'Can I play?' The children playing the game may say 'Yes' and then I may join the game.

The children playing the game may say 'No' and then I may play something else or be on my own. This is okay.

I am learning about joining a game.

What is a chasing game?

Mark loved being chased by other children. When he first started mainstream school he had little useful social language but quickly learned that if he pulled a face and said 'na-ni-ki-na-na!' the other children would chase him. This was a quick and successful way of producing a predictable reaction that he liked. It was his first foray into social interaction with neurotypical children outside his own family.

However, sometimes he became upset during a chasing game when he was caught and no longer chased. Children's games vary from day to day in the playground; each game is under the control of the child who initiates the game, the 'owner' of the game, and he or she decides what the rules for this game should be. This is an endlessly changing and complicated concept to teach a child with autism!

The very first Social Story™ was written by Carol Gray to describe the rules of a game 'Charlie over the water' to a pre-school student who was struggling to understand the game. It was so successful it began the whole strategy of Social Stories. Describing the rules of games in Social Stories is important because rules are frequently assimilated by the contextually aware neurotypical children, or described by other children in language that the very literal child is unable to completely understand.

A basic chasing game may be described in a Social Story, although the name of the 'chaser' may vary from 'it' to 'zombie' to whatever the fashionable idea is at the time. Before writing a Story about how a chasing game works I recommend that the author does some research on the vocabulary and rules of the current games being played in the individual child's playground. This will involve talking and drawing with more than one child! I was fortunate to have Mark's brothers to help me, so I had a ready source of information.

The first Story about chasing games needed to share information with Mark around the basic structure of a chasing game. As generalisation was a challenge for him, each time a new description of a game came into use, I would use this original Story as a master copy, a Story Master, from which others in a similar format could be made to build generalisation. As it is nearly impossible to keep abreast of the changing games in the playground, the Story later on also gave gentle guidance on how to ask about the rules when confused, and shared the very important information that it was okay to leave a game if the child is uncomfortable.

What is a chasing game?

Sometimes children play chasing games.
Usually one child is the chaser. The chaser runs
after the other children.

When the chaser touches another child
that child becomes the chaser. This is called
being caught.

Sometimes the chaser is called 'It' in the game. Sometimes the chaser is called 'Zombie' in the game. Sometimes the chaser is called something else. Usually when a child is caught he becomes the chaser and is called the chaser name.

Each chasing game may have its own rules. Sometimes this may be confusing. When I am unsure of the rules of a chasing game I may ask:

Sometimes I may like a chasing game. Other times I may dislike a chasing game. This is okay. I may stop playing whenever I feel uncomfy. I may play another game or play on my own. This is okay too.

I am learning about chasing games.

What does 'home' mean in a game?

This Story was written for a more specific situation. Mark came out of school one afternoon with a huge lump and bruise on his forehead, which he had acquired at break time in the playground. Helen, his LSA, told me that although she had not witnessed it, she had been told by the playground supervisor that Mark had become upset when he had been 'caught' in a chasing game and had deliberately banged his head against a wall. He had never done this before and everyone was very concerned. It was suggested that maybe another Social Story™ around winning and losing might help, although both Helen and I agreed that something else must have contributed to his distress, as this was a highly unusual behaviour for him.

When he was calm and rested the next day I explored it with a Comic Strip Conversation (page 34). This revealed that when Mark had been 'caught' by the boy doing the chasing in the game, he wanted to stop the game and walked away towards the playground fence. The boy then said, 'No Mark, you can't go home'. Mark's perspective of this comment, without understanding the context of the remark, was that he could never return home to his Mum, Dad, brothers, and all the things that made him comfortable and safe there. He believed that he would have to live at school from now on. This of course explained his response! I suggested to him that the boy may have been thinking that Mark, once caught, was not allowed *by the rules of the game* to return to the fence, which the children had called 'home' just for the duration of this game. It was an 'aha!' moment. The topic was discovered! I wrote the following Story, not about winning and losing, but about what 'home' means in a game. This Story was immediately successful because it made sense to Mark.

This experience was valuable because it taught me that I should never assume I know what my child's perspective is, just from my knowledge of autism or even my knowledge around *his* autism. There is always a need to observe, gather information and explore the perspective of the child. Had I not explored Mark's perspective with him, I would have written another Story about winning and losing. Mark may have become disengaged with Social Stories™ as they didn't seem relevant to him, and his trust in what I brought to him may have diminished. When the situation arose again, Mark's response would be unchanged and the assumption might then have been that maybe the Stories are not working any more, and *that* would have been a tragedy!

Time is always an issue for parents of children with autism and I freely admit that I too have written at least two Stories for Mark without exploring his perspective properly either in a conversation, or a drawing conversation. On both occasions I produced Stories that complied with all the Social Stories criteria, were meaningfully illustrated, and presented in an engaging way. Both did not harm him, because they adhered to the criteria, but neither made any difference to his response because I had not discovered the missing information he needed! Going back to the drawing board (literally) with Mark, I uncovered this information, rewrote the Stories and both were subsequently successful. I learned that time taken at the beginning to do thorough research, including talking or drawing with the child, saves time later spent unpicking the response and rewriting the Story.

When a child is able to communicate, authors should of course ask them, in whatever medium is comfortable for them, about their understanding of the situation. Using a Comic Strip Conversation is an effective way of doing this. Some children, however, are unable to communicate verbally and then we have to base what social information we need to share on our knowledge of their autism and how it may affect their understanding of a situation. However, to write effective Social Stories™ for this group of children, authors still need to observe and gather information carefully, consciously abandoning their own neurotypical assumptions. This is central to the Social Stories approach and the production of safe and effective Stories.

What does home mean in a game?

Sometimes children play chasing games.
Each chasing game may have its own rules.
Sometimes in a chasing game there is a place
where the chaser cannot catch other children.

This place may be called 'home' or 'base' for
this game, or it may be called something else.
Usually the children in the game decide where
'home' is at the beginning of the game. When a
child is standing in 'home', he cannot be caught
by the chaser. Children can rest from running
in 'home'.

Yesterday at break time we played a chasing game. The 'home' was the fence at the side of the playground.

When children were touching the fence the chaser could not catch them. When the game was finished the fence became just a fence again.

Sometimes a chasing game has no 'home'. This is okay too. When I am unsure of where 'home' is in a game I may ask:

Where is 'home' in this game, please?

I am learning what 'home' means in a game.

What does the whistle mean at break time?

In mainstream education in Year 1 at primary school Mark was required, like all the other children, to stop playing when the whistle was blown at the end of playtime and line up, before being 'dismissed' back to the classroom by the teacher. He found this confusing and simply did not comply. Mark had never been told exactly what the purpose of the whistle was, how different lengths of blow sent different messages and what the expected response was. He did not naturally copy the other children. I cannot be sure if the other neurotypical children were ever formally instructed in this either, as Mark had joined the school in the second year, but they certainly understood the context of the playground and where the whistle fitted in with its varied meanings. At the time Helen, his LSA, reported back that he carried on playing in a way that indicated he had no idea that the whistle was relevant to him. With a little encouragement he joined the line but did not appear to make a connection between the whistle and this response.

In fact, many children with autism and auditory hypersensitivity will move away from a sound because it causes them discomfort. They do not think to ask what it means, how long it will last, or if it can be reduced in volume, presumably because they are not mindful of what others know, so they seek their own resolution by running to the furthest point in the playground to escape the noise.

Of course, this avoidance behaviour may also be caused by a reluctance to return to the classroom where the re-entry and settling down of the class is a jostling, noisy affair, or because the task due after playtime is one they find meaningless or uncomfortable. Only by observing the situation carefully and talking with the child about it using a drawing conversation or Comic Strip Conversation (page 34) can the stimulus to the response be unpicked.

Having confirmed through a drawing conversation that Mark was unaware that the whistle had a message for him and the other children, I wrote the following Story which was immediately effective and the problem never arose again. The information was exactly what he needed to know – a hole in one!

It should be noted that every school will have its own particular method of bringing break time to a close. To use this Story for another child the author would need to observe the current practice at the school so that the information is accurate for that individual child.

When implementing the Story, a recording of the whistle can be incorporated initially at a low volume with a gradual increase in volume over time. I have used this technique successfully in the past with a Story about hand dryers.

What does the whistle mean at break time?

At school we usually have break time outside in the playground. A teacher is usually in charge of break time.

When a lot of children play outside they usually make a lot of noise. The teacher in charge of the playground has a whistle.

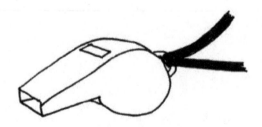

A whistle makes a loud noise. The whistle noise is loud so that children can hear it when they are playing.

Sometimes the teacher wants the children to stop what they are doing quickly. The teacher blows the whistle. One quick whistle (about one penguin) usually means that the teacher wants all the children to stop playing and listen to the teacher.

Another quick whistle (about one penguin) usually means the children may start playing again.

When playtime is finished, the teacher usually blows a long whistle (about three penguins).

This whistle usually means it is time to stop playing and line up.

I am learning about the whistle at playtime.

What is lining up?

In both primary and secondary school at the end of break time there is a signal, usually a bell or a whistle, that indicates that break time is finished and it is time to stop playing or chatting and line up.

Compliance with lining up may often be poor in children with autism. This may come from an underlying lack of understanding about lining up. The first difficulty begins with the term 'line up'. Is there a 'line down'? Neurotypicals automatically understand the likely context of this two-word phrase and its meaning, but actually the word 'up' here makes no sense at all for the child with autism who struggles to understand language that does not mean exactly what it says. So confusion begins with the introduction of this new skill to a child in language that lacks meaning for him.

There are many reasons why we ask people to line up – the most common one is because it is a fair way of giving everyone a turn at an activity or experience that only one person can do at a time. However, in the playground the reason for lining up is because it is a safe way to move a class back into school through the doorway, or along a corridor or up and down the stairs. If children did not line up and walk in line, there would be a huge crush of children trying to get through the doorway. Walking along in a line therefore allows children in one class to walk comfortably and safely past another class walking in a line along a corridor, through a doorway and up or down a staircase.

Mark did not respond to the whistle during or at the end of playtime and appeared to be unaware that the procedure had anything to do with him. I wanted to share social information around lining up with him and so I wrote two Social Stories™, one about the meaning behind the whistle (see the previous Story) and the other about the purpose of lining up and walking in lines.

To begin with I explored this at home with a series of drawings showing Mark how moving in lines stopped children bumping into each other. As he disliked being bumped into and preferred personal space around him he was particularly engaged with this new idea. I also described in a drawing that in order to move in a line the children had to *form* a line first. Then I showed him a line of three Lego® figures going into a doll's house through the front door and up and down the stairs, and how two lines of figures could pass by comfortably. As he seemed interested I then extended the example into real life, demonstrating that if he and I walked side by side through a doorway we would bump into his brother coming the other way, but if we went in a line, one behind the other, we could pass by without touching.

Having previously introduced the idea that the child's place in a line is usually dependent on *when* they join it, rather than their skill or ability, I was able to re-use this information within the 'What is lining up?' Story as it was already meaningful. The resulting Story brought clarity to the confusion around the request to 'line up'. It made sense! He immediately started to line up when the whistle was blown at the end of break time.

It is also important to consider that many children with autism have a different sense of proprioception to neurotypicals. They struggle to know where their body is in space. This may result in difficulty perceiving and understanding how to avoid physical contact with another person walking towards them. This difference in proprioception may explain the frequent bumps that our children experience, and why they may go on to interpret these sometimes as deliberate. A further Social Story™ explaining the unwritten rule of walking on the left helped too.

What is lining up?

A teacher usually watches break time to keep us safe. When break time is finished the teacher usually blows a long whistle. This means it is time to stop playing and stand in a line.

Standing in a line with one child behind another child is called lining up. Each class lines up together. This is okay.

When children walk in a line they may pass by another line of children without bumping each other. Walking in a line is a safe way for lots of children to move along corridors and through doorways.

Walking in a line is a safe way for lots of children to go back into school. To walk in line children need to stand in a line first. The teacher is pleased when the children line up.

Sometimes I will be at the front of the line.
Sometimes I will be at the end of the line.
Sometimes I will be somewhere in the middle.
This is okay.

My place in the line will depend on when I
joined the line.

I will try to line up at the end of break time. My teacher will be pleased with me

Who is in charge of
the playground?

One of the many admirable qualities in a child with autism is a strong sense of right and wrong. I have lost count of the times that Mark's clear black and white interpretation of the world has made me stop and rethink the many 'morally grey' stances we take in our modern world to explain away behaviour which is undoubtedly wrong.

This quality, however, has an inflexibility about it that makes it a problem in the playground when the child is trying to build friendships. A need to bring order to the confusing world around him, due to context blindness and a lack of mindfulness of others' feelings, may make a child with autism insist on everyone sticking to the rules. In the playground this may extend to the child assuming a policing role, trying to settle all playground disputes himself, which of course is unpopular with the other children and may lead to further isolation within his peer group.

Exploring this scenario with Mark in a drawing conversation revealed that he believed he was the best person to sort out troubles in the playground between other children. He was unaware that the adult supervising the playground was a more suitable person to deal with arguing children because she was an adult and had experience in handling children's disputes. It simply never occurred to Mark to ask for her help. There was a need therefore to share this information, so the following Story was written and also shared with the adult concerned so that they would be understanding of Mark's request to help. It was very successful.

Some schools have teachers supervising the playground as Mark's did at that time; many others have LSAs or other adult staff such as midday assistants. This Story can only be used if the supervising staff do know how to deal with children's disputes because a Social Story™ should always be truthful and accurate. Further Stories were written, later on, to address the more complex concept of 'dobbing in' friends, but initially relieving Mark of the job of policing the playground was a positive start.

Who is in charge of the playground?

Sometimes at school children play outside at break times. It is usually the teacher's job to watch the children in the playground and keep them safe. This is called being in charge of the playground. The teacher has been trained to be in charge of the playground.

Sometimes children have fun at playtime.
Sometimes children have arguments.
This happens when children play together sometimes. The teacher knows how to help children who are having arguments.

When I notice children having an argument I will try to tell the teacher. The teacher is the best person to help sort out an argument.

Other children usually listen to the teacher because they know the teacher is in charge of the playground. The teacher will be pleased with me.

Winning and
Losing

Stories about raffles

What is a raffle?

I was awesome at the raffle today!

At Mark's mainstream primary school there would frequently be raffles to raise money for charities and to increase the children's understanding of the need to think of others in less fortunate circumstances.

On each occasion Mark would become distraught if he did not win the prize. His LSA would take him out of the assembly when he became upset, and sometimes even before the raffle was drawn. Some staff felt his behaviour showed that he was spoiled and over indulged and very occasionally he would be gently told off for the upset he displayed.

In one school year the raffle would frequently be rigged to help him feel better. Although this was kind, it was not helping Mark to understand winning and losing and we had to respectfully explain that this may cause an unreal expectation of winning that could not be replicated in real life! He needed to experience raffles and competition but he also needed the same social information that everyone else had immediately at their fingertips, in order to control his response.

So that I could understand his response I attended an open assembly when parents were invited to come along. I was able to watch and note down how a raffle was introduced and conducted. I watched a wonderful toy being held up so that all the children could see it and the question asked, 'Who would like this toy? Tickets are 50p each!'

Mark was keen to buy a ticket and he, and many others, paid for tickets in their individual classrooms during the week. I asked to return the following week for the draw so that I could construct a Social Story™.

The next week when the much-coveted toy was given to another child who had the winning ticket, Mark looked confused and quickly became distraught. Looking around the assembly hall I was struck by the other children calmly clapping the winner, although undoubtedly feeling very disappointed themselves that they too had not won the prize. Every neurotypical child there completely understood the social concept of a raffle yet there had never been a lesson on 'How raffles work'. They also clearly understood that they were to hide their sad feelings and be a 'good sport' and clap the winner.

It was suddenly clear to me that without all this social information Mark would find it almost impossible to comply with these social rules. Because he was not mindful of other children's thoughts, wants or feelings, he would not have known that they all wanted to win the prize too. He may not have even observed others buying tickets either, and definitely did not know that tickets were being sold across the school in every classroom. In his literal thinking he had paid 50p for the toy and it was given to someone else. A gross injustice! Hard to bear, but compounded by the well-meaning telling-off that occasionally followed.

I noted down that even if Mark had looked at the other children around him he would have had absolutely no clues that they too were disappointed because they were looking completely calm while clapping the winner.

Later on at home while I was gathering more information from Mark through a Comic Strip Conversation about what had happened in the raffle he said, 'It isn't fair, I wanted the prize!' When I asked him if any of the other children wanted the prize he replied, 'No, they were clapping'. When I told him that every child who had bought a ticket wanted to win the prize he looked disbelieving. When I suggested to him that they may have been hiding their sad feelings when they were clapping it was an 'aha!' moment. The information he was missing was identified and Story topic discovered!

The following Story took a very long time to construct and there were many drafts. I discovered that describing how a raffle works was a difficult thing to do, but finally completed the Story and felt happy that it complied with the Social Story™ criteria. I bought several books of raffle tickets to concretely support the Story when reading it to him, by showing him what a raffle ticket looked like before it was taken from the book, and how an identical matching ticket remained in the book and then could be folded and put in a container. The school gave us warning of when the next raffle would be. I read the Story with Mark each evening, when he was calm and quiet, for seven days prior to the raffle, which was offering a large teddy bear as a prize. A copy was given to Helen, his LSA, who read it on the morning before the assembly. I made sure he was as well rested and relaxed on the morning of the raffle as possible. Then I waited with baited breath outside the school door for Helen to tell me how it went.

Mark's behaviour was reported to be much improved! Although still visibly upset, with tears running down his cheeks, he apparently clapped the winner of the bear and did not need to be taken out.

The minute we got home I wrote a praise story and we celebrated with him with Jaffa Cakes. We praised his effort of trying to hide his feelings, which demonstrated a new understanding, even though he had not been completely successful. Inclusion of the phrase 'I will try to hide my feelings' instead of 'I will hide my feelings' allowed us to do this. Praising effort and not just outcome is incredibly important with each Social Story™ and is easy to forget. Praise Stories are so powerful because they say what is assumed but sometimes not said – that the child did well to try to comply even if they did not manage to completely comply. Fifty per cent of all Social Stories™ written for a child should recognise the efforts and achievements of the child. This motivates the child to keep trying even when not immediately successful, thus building self-esteem (Howley and Arnold, 2005).

Mark has never developed an enjoyment of the anticipation of raffles, and is always bitterly disappointed when he loses, but he now has an understanding of the fact that others want to win too, and that there is a need to hide his disappointment and congratulate a winner, which is actually exactly what neurotypicals do!

Winning and losing continued to be a struggle for Mark throughout primary and into secondary school, but I never stopped trying to build his understanding with Social Stories. Years later, aged 19, he started college. He returned home after his first week and announced that the college was holding a competition for an iPad and that he had entered. My heart sank. I smiled an encouraging smile and asked him when the winner would be announced, thinking that I would need to find and rapidly update the raffle Story before then.

To my absolute astonishment and delight Mark peered closely at my face and said 'But don't worry Mum, I am prepared for disappointment!'

Thank you Social Stories!

What is a raffle?

A raffle is a game in which many people can buy a ticket with the same number written on it twice. People may buy one ticket or many tickets. All the tickets have different numbers.

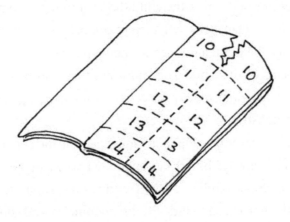

Usually each person who buys a ticket is given one half of the ticket with a number on it.

The job of the raffle is usually to collect money for a charity. All the money for the tickets sold is collected up and given to a charity.

On the day of the raffle all the other half-tickets are put in a container altogether. The container may be a bag, a box, a hat or maybe something else. Usually an adult or child is asked to pick out a half-ticket without looking at it.

Next the number of the ticket is called out so everyone can hear it.

The children and adults who have bought tickets usually look at their tickets. The person who has the same number ticket is the winner of the prize.

Sometimes there is one prize, sometimes two or three.

Mrs M is doing a Raffle for a teddy bear on Friday.

I have bought a ticket. Joe has bought a ticket. Bethany has bought a ticket. Tom has bought a ticket. Lots of children have bought a ticket.

I want to win the teddy. Joe wants to win the teddy. Bethany wants to win the teddy. Tom wants to win the teddy. Every child who has bought a ticket wants to win the teddy.

Only one girl or boy will win the teddy. Most of the other children will feel sad they have not won the teddy. They will try to hide their sad feelings. They may clap the winner of the teddy. They may think 'Maybe I will win next time'.

Sometimes I may win a raffle. Many times another boy or girl will win the raffle. This is okay. This is how raffles work.

On Friday I will try to stay calm if another boy or girl wins the teddy. I will work on hiding my sad feelings and clap the winner of the teddy.

Mrs M will be pleased with me. She may give me a sticker.

It is great to win a raffle. It is great to buy a ticket to help a charity too!

I was awesome at the raffle today!

This morning there was a raffle for a bear at assembly. The job of the raffle was to collect money for Children in Need. John won the teddy. I remembered to work on hiding my sad feelings and clapped the winner of the teddy. Mrs B was very proud of me. Mum was very proud of me too. Mum gave me a whole box of Jaffa Cakes! Mum told Dad I was awesome at the raffle today!

What is an award assembly?

Most primary schools have a reward programme that awards a certificate of some kind to a child who has worked hard that week. This is nearly always a challenging situation for a child with autism, and parents and teaching staff have frequently asked me if it can be addressed in a Social Story™. Mark always found award ceremonies difficult except when he was winning an award himself. Sometimes staff have expressed the opinion that when a child with autism exhibits a response like this it leads them to suspect he or she is over indulged at home and therefore is always expecting to win.

I usually first of all tell the staff about Mark and the school raffle (page 206). Although the raffle Story is a different scenario, it is a good example of the social information that is missing for the child with autism and the improvement in understanding that can be achieved with sharing that information in a Social Story™. In an award situation, however, the award is not randomly won by luck as in a raffle; the child has achieved something through effort which deserves acknowledgement, and so this is a different scenario, requiring different social information.

I encourage the parent or teacher to look again at the target situation from the perspective of the child with autism (I refer to this as putting on their 'Aspie specs'). A specific concrete award, usually in the shape of a certificate, is given to one child for working hard during the preceding week. This certificate is tangible proof that the teacher has recognised and is pleased that this child has worked hard that week. The child can hold it and see it whenever he chooses. He can show his parents and family. Compare this to words of approval that a teacher speaks. Words are transient in nature and quickly evaporate into the air, becoming invisible and, although the child can remember the person speaking them, he cannot revisit them when he wants to or remember them well enough to tell his family, particularly if he has poor social recall. A concrete reward is nearly always preferable to the child with autism to just verbal praise.

Children with autism are frequently hungry for approval, desperate to be noticed for doing the right thing, as they so frequently get things wrong socially and academically. Neurotypicals know that when a teacher is not correcting them that means she or he is usually happy with their progress. Because the child with autism is less able to accurately guess what is going on in someone else's mind, if that teacher is not stating they are pleased then they may not be pleased. However, if the teacher gives them a certificate there is no doubt!

Having recognised the significance of this concrete achievement for the child with autism, we must look beyond what is visible in order to unearth the social information needed to understand the situation – the information that is missing for the child with autism.

The teacher says this award is for hard work, and the child with autism knows he has worked hard. He may be oblivious to other children working hard, as due to lack of theory of mind he is unaware of what is going on in other children's minds. When the award is then given to another child, the child with autism may perceive this as an injustice and his response will display his frustration.

In fact, the teacher knows the child with autism is working hard too but the purpose of the weekly award is to stimulate *all* children to work hard. This is why the teacher tries to give the award to a different child each week to encourage each one of them. Faced with this situation we need to work out how much of this social information is available to the child with autism and then we need to provide what he is missing in a Social Story™. Exploring this with a Comic Strip Conversation is ideal. The teacher needs to reassure the child with autism that he knows he is working hard, and that this week the award is going to another child who is also working hard.

Once the Story has been introduced to the child it will need to be reviewed each time there is an award assembly until the child shows by his consistent response that it has become second nature to him. It should, however, never ever be enforced or read as a consequence for an undesired response. The child with autism may need this reminder to consider the neurotypical perspective because it may not be his innate thinking, just as we neurotypicals need reminding about the autistic perspective because it is not our innate thinking!

What is an award assembly?

On Fridays at school we usually have awards assemblies. At awards assemblies the headteacher, or another teacher, gives out the award certificate for hard work. There is only one winner each week.

Many children work hard at school. Many children want to win the award.

The teacher chooses a child who has worked hard that week. Sometimes I may win the award. Many times another boy or girl will win the award. This is okay. This is how the award certificate works.

My teacher knows I am working hard. My teacher wants to encourage other children to work hard too. This is why the award is given to a different child each week. This is a fair way of encouraging every child to work especially hard.

The headteacher or teacher reads out the name of the winner. Usually the winner feels happy and proud.

Many children feel sad and disappointed. They try to hide their sad feelings and clap the winner. Many children think 'Next time I may win'.

I will try to hide my sad feelings and clap the winner. Using my calming tools/strategies may help me. My teacher will be pleased with me.

I am learning about award assemblies.

What is a good sportsman?

In our culture it is usually expected that when games are played the winners and losers behave in a manner that keeps everyone comfortable. It is a general view that a gracious winner should not be boastful or celebrate in his opponents face out of respect for their feelings and comfort. We respect a gracious winner and call them a good sportsman. In the same way, a gracious loser should not be angry and resentful out of respect for his opponent's feelings and the comfort of the spectators. This too shows good sportsmanship and is something to be proud of. Human nature, however, drives winners to raise both arms, pump their fists and shout 'Yes!' when a match is won, sometimes in deliberate close proximity to the loser. However much we educate our children, whether with or without autism, to respond with good sportsmanship, there will always be those who will deliberately, or accidentally, cause unnecessary distress by their own response to winning.

It is unfortunate that the distress that occurs for children with autism when games are lost may be viewed by some neurotypicals with little sympathy and even with the general feeling that the child has been spoiled. While this may be the case in a few children with autism, the majority of children experiencing distress on losing a game are lacking fundamental information about what others' thoughts might be, what the general cultural feeling is around sportsmanship, and actually how to put that into place. From what I have observed over time, just telling a child 'not to be a sore loser and behave' does not usually cause any change in response, and neither does the deliberate exposure to repeated failures, but both may cause a further erosion of self-esteem. Missing social information needs to be shared, and safe and effective alternative responses gently suggested.

Mark and I, along with his LSA Helen and others, have worked hard on the concepts of winning and losing over many years and have found steady but slow progress emerging. Carol Gray suggests the idea of 'others like to play with good sports'. This is a simply brilliant focus to a Story on winning and losing and works really well because the child then has a reason to aim to become something else other than the winner. Sometimes, the motivation behind wanting to win comes from the desire to be noticed as relevant or valued, sometimes it is because the child wants the respect of others, but is unable to be successful socially and sees 'winning' as a clear way of people noticing him. If this is the case, sharing the idea of the respect others have for good sportsmanship can be very powerful.

I began to share the concept of good sportsmanship in a Social Story™, adding in the important but invisible social information about how others hide their disappointment. The important idea here is that others *continue to feel disappointed* inside but hide it with a formal method of showing good sportsmanship, i.e. that of congratulating the winner with a phrase like 'Well done', a handshake or clapping. Having a set procedure to follow gives a structure to think about while dealing with the sometimes overwhelming feelings of disappointment. We see this when a football team loses an important match and the players engage in a shaking of hands with the winners. At times of great anguish in life we all need structure to hold ourselves together!

It is important to note that negative words around losing are avoided in these Stories, and Mark's response to losing is also not described. I actively avoid the use of the words 'when I lose' because reading or hearing these words would engulf Mark in despair. To keep the Story positive and reassuring I use as much positive vocabulary as possible, so I choose 'when another child wins'. I never, ever, mention the undesired response of a child in the first person, in order to protect the child's self-esteem and engagement. Taking time to think about describing responses and events in positive language as we write eventually permeates the author's own communication. These days I naturally speak in positive, literal, accurate 'Social Story™' language with Mark. With a lot of practice, it has become second nature to me. I think that many authors who use Social Stories™ very frequently would agree that continually refining our choice of vocabulary and language in this way has had this effect on them too.

To support the following Story, Mark and I listened to family members expressing how much they too disliked losing but covered up their disappointment, despite continuing to feel it. We drew these conversations so he had plenty of time to look at the person's thoughts. If we were out and about and saw someone showing good sportsmanship in a game, I would comment on it to Mark. We examined TV footage of sports personalities displaying good sportsmanship and highlighted the commentator's remarks on their response, both within the footage and in the press. I cut out a post-it note in the shape of a thought bubble and stuck it next to the smiling photo of a footballer shaking a winning opponent's hand. On the post-it note was written 'I am disappointed...but I may win next time.' The Olympics and the World Cup football showed some fantastic examples both of good and poor sportsmanship! It is always good to have cultural ideas confirmed by independent *non-parental* parties.

What is a good sportsman?

Sometimes at school and at home children run races. Usually every child in a race wants to win.

Only one child can win the race. The other children are usually sad when another child wins. Many children hide their sad feelings and say 'well done' to the winner or clap the winner. They may think 'Next time I may win'.

Hiding sad feelings and saying 'well done' to the winner is called being a good sportsman. Other children like to play with children who are good sportsmen.

I will try to hide my sad feelings when another child wins the game.

I may say 'well done' to the winner. I may think 'Maybe next time I will win'. I am learning how to be a good sportsman.

What is a worthy opponent?

As Mark grew older and I learned more about his special interest, I was able to work on giving him a clearer mental picture of what good sportsmanship was, in a medium that was very meaningful for him and which he could quickly 'see' in his mind. To do this I drew from the popular video game lore that when the hero and the villain clash repeatedly, over time they may develop respect for the superior skill of the other. This is reflected in the higher score awarded for winning over a 'worthy' opponent. I illustrated this by reference to an episode of *Duel Monsters*, a favourite anime DVD he watched and also a game he played frequently. In one particular episode a player who has just lost his game congratulates the winning opponent on his skill. Using this example, I tried to show Mark that it was undoubtedly a more difficult challenge to beat those more skilled and experienced than yourself, and that therefore there was no dishonour in being beaten. The winning opponent was a 'worthy' opponent. This explained why the character who had lost congratulated his opponent on his winning moves. This was very helpful as it was a familiar and comfortable image that would pop into his mind when he was faced with this situation. I could even notice Mark's body posture changing as he 'saw' the image before him in his mind.

A sentence which will reliably bring to mind the essence of the Story is called a self-coaching sentence and is usually but not always connected to the child's special interest because this is so meaningful and important to him. In this Story, the self-coaching sentence was, 'It may help me to remember how in *Duel Monsters* when Yugi wins the duel with Mako Tsunami, Mako is disappointed but he accepts defeat honourably.'

Sometimes Mark would spontaneously choose a self-coaching sentence, and sometimes I would suggest one, based on his current special interest at the time.

I found the concept of winning and losing one of the most difficult to build, and both Mark and I have often felt our hearts sink with apprehension when a competitive game is suggested at social gatherings. However, just recently Mark told me, with genuine astonishment, that he had visited a friend, lost a game but actually hadn't minded because it was 'fun playing'. Something I thought I would never ever hear!

Please note that in the following Story, Mark's peer group are referred to as students to reflect their growing maturity.

What is a worthy opponent?

When students play games with other students, usually only one student or one team wins the game. Every student playing the game wants to win and is disappointed when another student wins. Many students hide their disappointed feelings and congratulate the winner.

It is easy to win a game when the opponent is less skilled at the game. It is a bigger challenge to win a game when the opponent is more skilled or experienced at the game. A skilled or experienced opponent may be called a worthy opponent.

When a worthy opponent wins many people think it is an honourable and respectful thing to recognise their skill. One way of doing this is to say, 'You were excellent – next time I will do better too!'

I will try to remember to recognise my opponent's skill. It may help me to remember how in *Duel Monsters* when Yugi wins the duel with Mako Tsunami, Mako is disappointed but he accepts defeat honourably. He tells Yugi that he had made some brilliant and unexpected moves.

What is my personal best?

A great deal of unhappiness is generated by trying to be 'better' than others. This philosophy underpins all competitive sport. A great deal of happiness can be generated by a closer focus on being the best one can be. This requires a shift in ideology. It is incredibly important for our young people with autism. Our young people need to be noticed and valued like anyone else. The winner of the race, the certificate or prize is *noticed* and applauded. Popular children at school are often the winners and there can be confusion between popularity, friendship and winning in children with autism.

I have discovered that teaching my son, and others, to use the concept of 'personal best' is a very successful way of helping them deal with winning and losing and feel comfortable. This applies to games of skill in sport, as opposed to games based on luck, but is also applicable to life in general.

Using real-life examples from the Olympics, I showed Mark how an athlete always notes his times after a race. The commentator often states that this is 'his personal best' for this race and may even say that although the athlete did not win, he did achieve a personal best and 'he will be pleased with that'. I then wrote a Social Story™ about 'What is my personal best?' in which I described how the most important thing in sport is to try to improve a performance. Recording his time, score or points each time he raced or took part in competitive sport allowed him to look back at his results over time. He could then concretely see if he had improved. If he had improved, even a little, he was moving closer to being the best he could be at that race or sport. This brought sense to competing with stronger competitors, as competing against those better than ourselves pushes us to exceed our personal best. It suddenly made losing a more positive experience and brought more sense to the 'taking part is fun'. It was also building the skill of positive self-reflection in a concrete way.

Winning and losing difficulties also surface in academic tasks in the classroom. Children with autism of high ability frequently have unrealistically high expectations of themselves academically and struggle when they fail to achieve 100 per cent in class tests. I have used this personal best strategy successfully for class spelling tests, mental mathematics tests and later on in school for public examinations. Of course, sometimes results do not improve by even a point and in these situations we look at how the *average* scores are improving over time.

Of all the winning and losing Stories this has been the most successfully shared with others, and some parents have also had success using the personal best strategy in situations such as getting dressed in the morning, timing how long it takes and recording it in a personal best book!

It is also incredibly applicable across the lifespan. Years after finishing school and college, Mark wanted to take up the sport of fencing. Initially he began with a tutor on a one-to-one basis who taught him, at his own pace, the required basic skills of fencing. His tutor suggested he joined the local fencing club that met twice a week not far from our home. During the course of an evening at the fencing club, each fencer will fence other club members. So Mark had to learn to cope with several fencing matches during an evening, which due to his lack of experience as a novice fencer he was likely to lose. I reintroduced the personal best Story again and provided him with a personal best book to write in his scores so that out of each match he could find some improvement in his points gained, no matter how small. This was immediately successful.

I also wrote a Social Article demonstrating the specific experience and training of three fencers at the club – giving concrete, indisputable facts about how practice over many years had honed their skills. This showed him why they were difficult to beat and two years on, this Article, combined with his personal best strategy, is still working well for him. This has allowed him to improve his skills at fencing and begin to realise his potential at the sport, and that in turn allows him to be part of the social aspect of belonging to an adult sports club.

What is my personal best?

Sometimes at school we have races.
Sometimes I win, sometimes another student
wins. This is okay, this happens to everyone
from time to time.

The important thing in racing is to try to
improve. Great athletes try to improve their
performance each time they race. Usually their
coach times how long it takes the athlete to
run the race with a stopwatch.

The best time the athlete achieves is called their 'personal best', or PB for short. Racing against strong competitors pushes athletes to improve their personal best. Many great athletes like Usain Bolt feel pleased when they improve their personal best time even if someone else wins the race.

I may write down my time for each race in a special PB notebook. The best time I achieve will be my personal best.

I may feel pleased if I improve my personal best even if someone else wins the race. Improving my personal best means I am moving closer to being the best I can be at that race. My coach will be pleased with me.

Stories about Markachu II's chill attack

The story of Markachu II's chill attack

When to use my chill attack

Winning and losing remained a challenge for Mark throughout his school days. After sharing other children's thoughts and wishes in the 'What is a raffle?' Story (page 210) there was a definite improvement in raffle situations; however, coping with winning and losing in games lessons and ultimately at the school sports day in a public arena was a much greater challenge.

Following our initial work on the emotion of calm, Mark had a concept of what calm felt like for him and what tools to use to self-calm if he was unsettled by unexpected changes or events (page 56). He was frequently able to identify unexpected changes and implement his calming tools successfully. But occasionally, when other children said things deliberately to unsettle him he was less successful in recognising their intention and therefore employing his calming tools. To tackle this difficult area of identifying intentions I decided to use familiar and comfortable constructs that he could identify with. I used Mark's strong love for the colour blue along with his interest in Pokemon® to write a Story addressing this valuable information.

Using the special interest to engage and focus a child with autism is now recognised as an effective strategy in the classroom and it is commonly used by both parents and professionals as a distraction, reward or incentive. It may also be incorporated into the actual academic curriculum to engage with a learning task with good effect. The special interest may also be used to make the unpalatable subject of 'social' more engaging and meaningful in a Social Story™. However, there is a careful balance to be struck, as the message of the Story may be easily overshadowed by reference to the special interest, unless the use of it is integral and meaningful within the Story content. I discovered an effective method of achieving this for Mark. I noted that, like many other children with autism, he connects with specific characters within his special interest, being able to copy their voice, intonation and body movements exactly. It is as though, for a few moments, he almost becomes the character. The characters in these stories exhibit emotions in a very clear way. Mark can recognise that emotion easily and perhaps that is why he uses lines of script and the body gestures and postures from those scenarios to represent what he is feeling. He was doing this for characters that exhibited very clear large-scale emotions. If this is how he was expressing his emotions to me it made sense that I should try to use the same medium to help him identify characters that are, for example, feeling unsettled but managing to control their emotion using a calming tool or cue. These may be less easy for him to recognise initially, but once highlighted to him would be a powerful visual image for him to refer back to.

As a starting point I gathered information from games lessons where Mark became distressed when he lost the ball in a football or rugby match. Most children were very understanding of Mark's difficulties at school, but a couple had learned how to unsettle him with a single comment. Once unsettled, his football or rugby skills quickly foundered. We explored this together using a Comic Strip Conversation, which demonstrated that Mark was unaware of their thoughts or the intentions behind their comments.

I wanted Mark to feel supported by a team of people and to have an instantly accessible strategy at times of imminent stress. I decided on using a two-word cue 'chill attack' to help him to recognise the situation he was in, and recall the Story message. It was a familiar kind of phrase similar to those heard in Pokemon® storylines. I then wrote a story describing an invented Pokemon character called Markachu II being trained in touch rugby by a team of trainers including Mumathon, Barkerathon, Trollopathon and Newcomathon. It was easy for him to identify with these characters, because they were obvious caricatures of his Mum, Helen Barker his LSA, and Mr Trollope and Mr Newcombe, who were his two games teachers at his school.

The opponents were represented in the Story as Team Zocket, and bore strong resemblance to Team Rocket, the 'baddies' in the Pokemon series. Team Rocket's intentions are always very clearly unfriendly in the usual Pokemon storyline. My story explained how Team Zocket might deliberately choose to unsettle Markachu II so as to give them an advantage in a game. It then described how employing his 'chill attack', which contained his calming tools, allowed him to perform well and outsmart their cunning plan. I drew Markachu II in Mark's favourite colour blue, and changed the colour to red to illustrate when Markachu II was unsettled by his opponents. When his calming tools were engaged, a picture showed how the red colour drained away from him returning him to his original shade of blue.

Mark's 'calming tools' included feeling his hanky which was sewn into his pocket, counting penguins, and recall of his hero dealing with a challenge (page 56). Initially these were pictured here as a visual prompt to link him back to his calm Story. Later on he no longer needed the visual link so they are not pictured in this version.

'The story of Markachu II's chill attack' was read initially as a simple fictional story and Mark absolutely loved it! Because it is not true, I cannot call it a Social Story™. However, I then wrote a Social Story to explain how he could use this story to remind himself of what to do when he began to feel unsettled in a game. This 'story within a Story' format was a one-off but it does show how the child's interest can be used to explain concretely the 'unfriendly' intentions of others without making the child lose self-esteem, giving him a vivid mental image of how to deal with feeling unsettled by others. It was very meaningful for Mark at the time and also helped him when we were out and about. The two words 'chill attack' quickly cued Mark into the Story when other children were deliberately unsettling him, allowing him to recognise the context he was in.

Using fictional characters to help understand emotions and emotional regulation is not new. Here, however, I am actively searching the child's own individual special interest for characters and language that are meaningful and comfortable for him. I think that this takes the sting out of a difficult topic and encourages the engagement of the young person.

This fictional story, however, obviously requires an understanding of symbolic representation, and analogy, which other children with autism may or may not have and so although a good example of the power of story and Social Stories™, it is not suitable for all. Many years later I was writing Stories about intentions again in a different format for Mark and other students. These are featured earlier in the book (page 109).

The following story was originally in colour, but is reproduced here in black and white

The Story of Markachu II's chill attack

Markachu II is a cool blue type of Pokemon from the Pikachu family.

He evolved from the Markachu I Pokemon and his greatest strength is his chill attack.

Markachu II goes to a great Pokemon training school. This school has two famous trainers called Newcomathon and Trollopathon who have trained many champion Pokemon. These school trainers joined forces with Markachu II's personal trainers Barkeramon and Mumathon to make an awesome training team.

The team are training Markachu II in touch rugby at the famous Pokemon Stadium.

When Markachu II is calm and in control he is a cool blue colour. When calm and in control Markachu II is a great player of touch rugby. When Markachu II begins to lose control his colour changes to red.

Markachu II has a chill attack made of calming tools which calm him down and change his colour from red back to cool blue. The training team's mission is to train Markachu II to employ his chill attack so that he stays calm and in control.

Team Zocket, the opponents, know that when Markachu II is unsettled his play weakens. This helps them win the game. Team Zocket know what words to say to unsettle Markachu II.

Team Zocket say the words. Markachu II's blue colour begins to fade away and he becomes red. His play begins to weaken.

His trainer quickly calls 'Markachu II, Chill Attack!' This reminds Markachu II to employ chill attack.

Markachu II employs full chill attack. His red colour fades away and he becomes blue again. Markachu II is in control, calm and blue once again! Look out Team Zocket!

When to use my chill attack

The story of Markachu II's chill attack is a story about a pretend character called Markachu II. In the story, Markachu II becomes unsettled in a game. Sometimes in real life players become unsettled in a game. Sometimes even great champions can be unsettled in a game.

When Markachu II is unsettled he uses his chill attack to become calm and in control again. When I am unsettled in a game my chill attack may help me become calm and in control again.

When I am calm and in control of my skills I am a better player. My coach will remind me when to use my chill attack. It may help me to think about the Markachu II story. I am learning about when to use my chill attack.

School Events

Sports day happens once a year

Sports Day is frequently a very challenging day for children on the autism spectrum. It involves complete disruption to the timetable involving a different place, uniform and activities to normal. The children are placed often in 'houses', a concept many children with autism find difficult to understand, and which is frequently not explained in sufficient detail. There is a lot of random noise: clapping, cheering, whistles and bells. The day consists of numerous races that involve coping with tactile jostling with other children, winning and losing, and social interaction. All of this is observed by parents and teachers. There is huge pressure to perform, if not as a promising athlete then at the very least as a good sportsman.

I used to give Mark perspective of the idea 'once per year' by colouring in the date for sports day on the wall planner calendar on the kitchen wall which concretely showed him how infrequently it occurred. I would always work especially hard on his self-esteem in the weeks running up to sports day, defining his strengths, commenting on them and writing praise Stories around them. I would try to point out how other children in the class had different strengths and weaknesses too. On the evening following sports day I would write a praise Story for his effort which he would show his Dad when he came home, along with photos of positive moments, and I would ask nothing of him other than allowing him restorative solitude if he wanted it. The next available day we would take part in a fun activity of his choice.

If asked now by school staff and parents for tips on how to help the day pass well, I have the following advice. It is useful to establish a 'personal best' philosophy early on in the year and then refresh and reinforce this in the summer term with qualifying or practice races. Comparison to famous athletes or sports figures the child is familiar with will help clarify this. A personal best Social Story™ for the child and a personal best (PB) notebook to record their times and scores is ideal (page 237).

Thinking ahead about the sensory side of sports day and factoring in sensory relief is very important, for example allowing earphones or ear defenders, a peaked cap or shades. Allowing a sensory toy to be accessible in the child's pocket or giving him access to a sensory relief area when overwhelmed and a non-verbal method of requesting this is also ideal. Teaching strategies for big or small 'body breaks' can really help a child with sensory needs. There are many excellent examples of these for children who seek sensory input to self-regulate in Lauren Brukner's book *The Kids' Guide to Staying Awesome and In Control*. Some of these may be used in a warm-up session and some while sitting cross-legged on the grass!

I also suggest that any Stories are shared with the parents so that there is consistency between home and school. After the day is over, I advise that photos of the day, along with successful Social Stories, are placed in a 'sports day' resource for the following year. I encourage all parents to help their child with self-reflection on their effort on the day and to place photos of their child during and after the day in their home resource for sports day for next year. A praise Story from parents for effort is so important too!

My Social Story for sports day would share with Mark what the plan was for the day, including details of where he would sit (using information from Helen, his LSA), where I would be, and what I would be wearing to make myself easy to spot in the crowd (e.g. a red cap), also what the order of the races would be, and when lunch would take place. I emphasised what would be the *same,* for example he would still have the same lunchbox, go to school at the same time and return home at the end of the day. I also wrote a Story about change of plan, for example if it rains where the children would go, what the plan B would be, and importantly who would know and tell him about Plan B. Reviewing previous Stories about calm (page 56) personal best (page 234) and sportsmanship (page 224) to refresh his understanding of these difficult concepts was also important as the Story for sports day concentrated only on what was to happen on the day.

The best illustrations here are photographs, but obviously this is difficult for the first time the child experiences sports day. I have put drawings where a photo used to be to give an idea of the layout and format of the Story.

Sports day is often the time for less academic sporty children to shine, and on prize day it is the turn of the academic non-sporty children to have their moment. The school concert allows those with musical and acting talents to have their time in the spotlight. If, however, your child is not academic, sporty, musical or dramatically talented, and in addition, finds the social arena and friendships difficult to navigate, these occasions will be miserable and self-esteem will inevitably take a tumble. It takes compassion and imagination from staff to work out how to incorporate the talents of those with autism into these events. I have heard heart-warming reports from some parents of staff actively building self-esteem by assigning a student with autism the important role of time recorder in a race, or involving him in the production and distribution of programmes to parents and visitors. This takes precious time and energy to set up and supervise at a time when there are so many demands on teaching staff, but the benefit to the student with autism may be immense.

Sports day happens once a year

Sports day usually happens only once a year in the summer term.

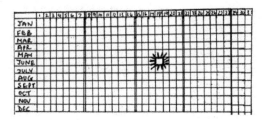

My school has sports day scheduled for next Wednesday.

MONDAY	TUESDAY	WEDNESDAY	THURSDAY	FRIDAY
Maths	Science	↑	German	PHSE
Maths	Science		German	PHSE
English	History	SPORTS	French	History
English	Geog		Science	History
English	Geog	DAY	Science	Geog
	L U N C H		B R E A K	
Art	German		Science	PE
Art	French		Science	PE
Art	French	↓	English	PE

Sports day is a day when the usual timetable is replaced by another timetable just for that day. When sports day is finished, the timetable is back to normal the next day.

On sports day the children usually have many kinds of races and sporting events. Sports day happens at the games field. The day usually begins about the same time as any other school day. The day usually finishes about the same time as any other school day.

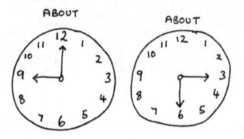

I will have my lunch from my lunchbox just like any other school day.

Mrs B usually helps me on sports day just like any other school day. Mrs B knows how to help me.

On sports day children usually wear their sports kit to school. Between races the children in Romans house usually sit together near the red flag on the grass. Red is the colour for the Romans house. Mrs B or another adult will show me where to sit.

On sports day I am scheduled to be in the high jump and the 800m race.

Sometimes it rains on sports day and there is a change of plan. Mrs B will tell me if there is a change of plan and what the new plan is. This is okay.

Mum is planning to watch sports day. Mum has chosen a red cap so that I may easily see where she is sitting.

Mum will cheer me on when I am in my race. She will bring a stopwatch and time my race. If my personal best time has improved, Mum will wave a red scarf.

Children usually cheer when a child from their house is in a race. This is called supporting their house. When I am not in a race I may support my house too.

When sports day has finished, Mum will take me home. When we get home I may have a bath and watch my favourite DVD. The school timetable will be back to normal on Thursday. Sports day usually happens only once a year.

What are the four houses at school?

Within Mark's school there were four houses: Romans, Saxons, Normans and Danes. Each house had its own house colour and a house captain. The children wore school ties in the colour of their allocated houses. Because the majority of children were neurotypical there never was any reason to explain the system in great depth because the children assimilated this information easily from minimal instruction. As sports day often included an emphasis on the 'houses' the children belonged to, this needed to be explained in a Social Story™ too. Without this information the child with autism might be confused as to why he is expected to cheer for the Romans!

The Story identified five other children in each of the houses in order to give him a reference point of who belongs where. This may be problematic for a very literal child who may need more detail, but it worked well for Mark.

What are the four houses at school?

My school has four 'houses'. The names of the houses are – Romans, Normans, Saxons and Danes. The word 'house' usually means a building. The word 'house' in school may also mean a group of children. In my school each student is given a house name. This is called 'belonging' to a house. My brothers and I belong to Romans house.

ROMANS HOUSE

NORMANS HOUSE

SAXONS HOUSE

DANES HOUSE

Each house wears a different colour tie so that others can see what house they belong to. I wear a red tie because red is the Romans house colour and I am in the Romans house.

Our games kit has our house colour on the collar and sleeves of the t-shirt. On sports day the winner from each race collects points for their house. The house with the most points is the winning house. The captain of that house will receive the cup for all the children in that house. The cup will usually have ribbons in the winning house colour on it.

Winning the cup is an honour for all the children in the winning house. This is the reason children cheer on their house. They are trying to encourage all the children in their house to do their best.

I am learning about the four houses at school.

What is a swimming gala?

Once a year the school would have a swimming gala. This took place at a local swimming pool where the children usually had their swimming lessons. Swimming lessons are frequently a source of great distress to children with autism. It is not difficult to see why when we abandon our own perspective and think about the experience from their perspective.

A high percentage of children with autism may experience sensory dysregulation which means they may be unable, or less able, to fade unwanted sensations into the background to let them concentrate on the sensations relevant for that situation. Sensations that are commonplace for the neurotypical children may cause discomfort or even pain for the child with autism.

Swimming pools have dreadful acoustics, with even the smallest noise ricocheting around the walls and the surface of the water, so the noise of excited children's chatter can be overwhelming for a child with autism. In a swimming lesson the teacher also needs to shout so all the children can hear and often uses a shrill whistle. The strong smell of the chlorine, the proximity of large numbers of children jostling for a place in the line by the pool, and the pressure of arm bands blown up to stay on arms, combined with the speedy need to undress into a swimsuit make the pool environment a recipe for disaster. This all happens within a completely different social context to the classroom or school. Within the swimming lesson, the child in the pool may or may not understand the teacher's directions because of his literal understanding of language, and even if he does have the understanding, he may struggle with the co-ordination and proprioception required to make his body copy the swimming teacher's requests or actions. It is absolutely no surprise that this poses difficulties for those with autism. What surprises me more is that they are able to navigate the environment at all! On top of all this sensory stimulation the swimming gala introduces a competitive element, combining a pressure to perform well in the sport with an expectation to show good sportsmanship, just like on sports day. This occurs in the presence of a crowd or parents, whose applause and chatter ramps up the volume of uncomfortable noise in a confined space.

Mark dreaded the swimming gala. He found the noise almost unbearable and frequently had his fingers in his ears. However, he was most happy in the water, which he had loved since he was very tiny, possibly because the even pressure of water all over his body made him feel secure and comfortable. He had swimming lessons each week outside school and was learning breaststroke and crawl with me in the water beside him, translating the instructor's words. At the school swimming lesson and gala he had no translator in the water with him, but on the poolside Helen always knew when he was struggling to understand and would step in to help him cope whenever necessary.

A Story addressing the noise at swimming lessons outside school had been written and Mark knew why it was so noisy, how long the noise would last and how he could reduce it for himself. To write the Story about the gala I gathered information as best I could. For the first Story I tried to predict what would be challenging for him, given that he had never experienced a swimming gala before, and then I used my understanding of his perspective. It worked to a point, but there were details I had not included in sufficient detail.

After attending the first gala I was able to add these details as I had seen first-hand what happened and was able to make a good guess about how Mark felt at each stage during the competition, as I had observed his response.

The huge support Mark received from Helen during events like sports day and the swimming gala was clearly evident and her contribution to the outcome was invaluable.

We celebrated his effort when he got home with a Jaffa cake tea (just Jaffa Cakes!) and a praise Story which I wrote inside a congratulations card. Before bed we looked together at the wall planner and noted that the swimming gala would not be happening for another year.

What happens at a swimming gala?

My school has a swimming gala once a year.
The swimming gala is planned for next Monday.
The gala is a swimming competition for all the
junior children.

On Monday morning buses will take the junior
school children to the swimming pool. Mrs B will
be coming too. Many mums and dads will be at
the pool to watch the gala.

There are lots of swimming races at the gala.
Some children swim fast. Some children swim
slowly. This is okay.

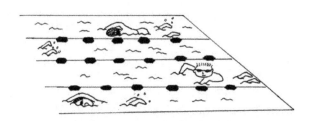

Joe and I are swimming in races with lots of other children. I want to win my race. Joe wants to win his race. All the children in a race want to win.

The mums and dads clap and cheer the children. My Mum will be at the gala. My Mum will be clapping and cheering us too.

Lots of children swim in the races. Only one child can win a race. The other children usually feel disappointed when another child wins. Many children hide their sad feelings and think 'Maybe I will win next time'. Sometimes they say 'well done' to the winner. This is called being a good sportsman.

Many people respect winning swimmers and many people respect good sportsmen too.

I will try to hide my sad feelings when another child wins a race. I may think 'Maybe I will win next time'. I may say 'well done' to the winner. I am learning how to be a good sportsman.

My Mum will be proud of me and cheer me. Mrs B will be proud of me and cheer me too.

When my race is finished I will try to wait patiently until all the races finish. I may cheer and clap the children in my house to encourage them to do their best too.

When all their races are finished the children get dry and changed. When the teacher says it is home time Mum will take me home for some Jaffa Cakes!

Stories about the school trip

What is the plan for my school trip?

What happens when there is a change of plan?

School trips are organised to give children confidence at being away from home, and experiences as a group that they may not necessarily have at home or school. They are considered to be an important part of the curriculum and every child is encouraged to attend. The problem for children with autism is that experiencing new activities in unfamiliar places, with a group of other people, far from normal routine, is a recipe for anxiety and distress. However, it does not necessarily need to be, provided adequate research and preparation are carried out, and Social Stories™ are written and read with the child before the trip.

Before any school trip Mark would make with the school I would try, where possible, to visit the place beforehand so that I was informed enough to write a Social Story™ for him about the visit. Often places were very approachable and accommodating when I explained the reason for my visit.

Understanding the perspective of the child with autism and predicting what might be difficult for him is very important in gathering information for a Story. I would begin by noting the time taken to travel there and compare it to the length of one episode of my son's current favourite TV programme. Bringing my camera, I would photograph all areas at the venue where the group of children would be likely to go, not forgetting quiet areas where Mark might need to be withdrawn to in the event of rain changing an outdoor activity into a noisy indoor activity.

I also photographed all the possible activities where they would eat their lunch, the toilet block, the car park and the gift shop. While looking around I would carry out a quick assessment of the sensory environment checking out the noise and light levels during activities and sensory experiences and making a note to bring supports that might be required such as earphones, shades or a peaked cap. Once during a pre-school visit to a local castle I noted a 'reality' experience with sound and visual effects of people being trapped in a burning temple. It would have been completely overwhelming for Mark and this information helped his LSA steer him away from this exhibit and focus him on one with similar information but without the sensory overload.

When it was impossible for me to visit the place or find information I tried to ensure that Mark was accompanied by his LSA who understood how he perceived the world, and who I knew would keep him comfortable so that he could gain as much as he could from the experience.

Nowadays a destination can be identified online and the time it takes to travel there calculated. An interactive virtual trip can even be made via the destination website.

However, legislation requires schools to carry out risk assessments for outings, and a member of staff is usually sent to carry out a health and safety visit at the school trip destination. The paperwork for this is extensive and time consuming, but it is an ideal opportunity for that member of staff to put on a pair of 'Aspie specs' and take the child's perspective while looking around, gathering all the information and photographs needed for a Social Story™.

The Stories written for Mark would contain a lot of information about what would be the same as any other school day as well as what would be different. This is helpful for a child with autism, who will focus mostly on what is different about the day. Within the text it did not say he 'will' enjoy the activities because this was an unknown at this point. It was full of the detail he required and lots of reassuring repetition. Sometimes neurotypicals find the repetition boring within a Social Story but many children with autism find it comforting and like the feeling of predictability it brings.

Transporting large groups of children on school trips rarely goes without a hitch and inevitably something unexpected happens to the plan for the day. Weather and traffic are the usual culprits but sickness is also frequently a factor, causing a teacher or LSA to be unexpectedly absent. So along with the Social Story™ 'What is the plan for my school trip?' I wrote another with the title, 'What happens when there is a change of plan?' to share with Mark what possible changes might occur, who would know what the new plan was, and how to remain calm.

When a school writes a Story to prepare a child for a school trip I recommend that afterwards the Story is placed in a 'school trip' special needs department resource file, along with notes on any strategies that were particularly helpful, such as 'headphones were very helpful as it is extremely noisy when it rains and children are inside'. In my experience schools tend to use the same destinations year on year, particularly if the first is successful, and if so this will help save time for the next child who needs it. Of course, each Story will still need to be individualised for each child, and a check should always be made that details about the destination hold true before introducing it to another child with autism the following year.

If a member of staff writes a Story for a child, it is really helpful to share it with parents, who ideally should be consulted about its contents. First, it can be regularly reviewed at home in the run up to the trip, ensuring consistency. Second, it can be a good resource for parents to use to reflect on with the child after the event, building their confidence in their achievement. It may also highlight supports needed for the day, such as a peaked cap and earphones, which the parents can then encourage the child to have ready.

Doing research about the trip and the likely activities also highlights any new vocabulary that may be used on the day by guides or instructors. It is really helpful if these terms are explained in a literally accessible way to the child with autism, before the trip, so he will understand their meaning just as all the other children will. This is very important for safety instructions on activity trips!

It is helpful too if accompanying staff try not use language, at least within earshot of the child with autism, that could cause distress because of the child's very literal a-contextual understanding. An example of this might be an adult exclaiming, 'We'll never get home!' when looking out the coach window at the traffic jam – one of the most upsetting comments a literal child with autism can ever hear on the coach journey back home!

Independence and resilience are built on the confidence that comes from successfully navigating challenges, not from being bulldozed through a distressing experience. Children with autism may need support to navigate the day, and a Social Story™ is an ideal way to help provide this, along with adequate understanding and supervision. It is important not to avoid all challenges but to support the child through them so that they are empowered for the next one that comes along. A successful experience can lead to enthusiasm for future trips for both staff and child!

What is the plan for my school trip?

On ... my class is going on a school trip with Mrs B and our teachers. We are going to ... This story tells me the plan for my school trip.

At my school, children usually wear school uniform. On our school trip children wear home clothes. Wearing home clothes on a school trip may help me feel comfy.

On Monday I will go to school at about the usual time, just like on a normal school day.

I will bring my packed lunch, just like on a normal school day. My lunch will be the same as on a school day.

About 9am a coach will arrive at school to take us to .... All my class, my teachers and Mrs B and I will get on the coach. The coach usually looks like this photo.

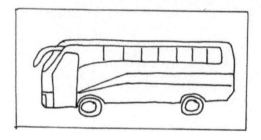

I may sit in a window seat or another seat. I may sit next to Mrs B or another child. All children and adults on a coach usually wear seat belts just like in a car. This keeps the children and adults safe on the coach.

The coach journey to ... usually takes about one hour. This is as long as one episode of NCIS.

On the coach journey I may:

play with my Nintendo Game Boy or

listen to my music with my headphones or

look out the window or maybe do something else.

When the coach has arrived and parked at... it will be time for everyone to get off the coach.

Mrs B may help me find a safe place to put my bag and coat. If I need to use the toilet Mrs B will help me find one.

Then there will be activities outside. Here are some photos of the activities. There may be other activities too, and this is okay.

Many children enjoy these activities. These activities may be fun for me too. An adult will tell the children how to do the activities.

If I need help Mrs B will show me how to do the activities. She knows how to help me.

When the activities are finished it will be lunchtime. I may choose to eat my lunch with Mrs B or another child.

After lunch we will do more activities. Here are photos of some of the afternoon activities. There may be other activities too, and this is okay.

Many children enjoy these afternoon activities. These afternoon activities may be fun for me too. An adult will tell us how to do the activities. If I need help Mrs B knows how to help me.

When the activities are finished it will be time to go to the gift shop and buy one souvenir. I have £5 to buy a souvenir.

When all the children have finished buying their souvenirs it will be time to go back to school. We will collect our bags and coats. I may use the toilet before the journey home if I want to. Then everyone on our school trip will get back on the coach.

I may sit next to Mrs B or another child. All the children and adults usually wear seat belts on the coach to keep them safe.

When the coach gets back to school it will soon be time to go home. My teacher or another adult will tell us when we can go home.

Mum will be waiting in the playground in her usual spot. Mum will be pleased to see me. This story tells me what the plan is for my school trip.

What happens when there is a change of plan?

On Monday I am going on a school trip with my LSA Mrs B, my class and my teachers. The teachers and Mrs B have a plan for my school trip. Sometimes unexpected things happen to a plan.

Sometimes the weather changes what we do. We may do another activity. This is okay. Mrs B will tell me what the activity is. She knows how to help me.

Sometimes traffic changes our journey times. We may take longer to travel. This is okay. We will still go home at the end of the day. Mrs B will tell me the approximate time we will get home.

Sometimes a teacher or an LSA is sick and someone else goes with us. This is okay. I will have someone with me who knows how to help me.

When something unexpected happens I will try to stay calm and ask an adult what the new plan is. Staying calm when there are unexpected changes is a clever thing to do. Staying calm helps my brain think. I may use my calming tools to help me stay calm.

My teacher will be pleased with me if I try to stay calm when there is a change of plan. She may give me a sticker.

I am moving up a level to Year 3

We experience transitions everyday throughout our life. We move seamlessly from mother's knee to playschool, from playschool to nursery, from nursery to primary school, from primary school to secondary school, from secondary school maybe to further education and from there into our first workplace. At the same time, within each of the above categories transitions are taking place between daily events from getting out of bed, to getting dressed, to leaving the house, to travelling to work and so on.

Throughout life our bodies are also undergoing transitions each day as we 'morph' from baby into toddler, from toddler into child, from child into youth, from youth into adult and from adult into elderly adult. We are constantly having to adapt to our new body form. Our relationships too are in constant transition as we expand our roles from being a child to a sibling to a friend, a best friend and eventually a partner and maybe even a parent ourselves.

Life is a continuing set of transitions and we neurotypicals are fortunate that our social understanding enables us to cope with the changes that these transitions bring.

Children with autism, however, have a different social understanding, and with less context and sensitivity and weak central coherence they are less able to work out the general 'gist' (the context) of a situation and to focus on the relevant social clues, choosing instead to focus on clues that are non-contextual but of interest to them. The relevant social clues are crucial for understanding what that situation is, how it is likely to pan out and what behaviour and language to select to be safe and effective within that situation. Without these processes working well for them, children with autism may struggle with small changes to any situation and may try to keep everything the same so that they can predict what is coming next, understand expectations and feel safe.

Within the timetabled structure of the school day Mark was able to predict what was coming next, when it would start and finish, and what was expected of him. He was comfortable in a familiar context; however, when inevitable school day changes popped up, like a supply teacher, a surprise test, a change in the timetable, he became quickly confused and upset. Visual timetables helped tremendously and we had one at home too. As he grew older I made him a personal visual timetable by slotting cards into a business card holder in a personal organiser. Each card depicted what the lesson was with a picture and a word. Over time the pictures were no longer required and it became a written timetable. I introduced a 'COP' card within the visual timetable, which we called a 'change of plan' card that was slotted in when there was to be a change. This was introduced very slowly, at home, making the change something better than the original planned activity at first and then slowly allowing the change to become something less desirable, but with a positive activity visible on the timetable for after the change.

With the finish of every school year came of course the long summer holiday, at the end of which inevitably came massive transition and change. Mark's teacher, classroom and timetable changed. His books, subjects and homework changed. His classmates sometimes changed too. He used different toilets and hung his coat on a different hook in a different place. Anxiety with all the change could become overwhelming.

Early preparation with shared information about the coming changes in the form of a Social Story™ transition book really helped. It was clear from Mark's perspective that the yearly transition would always be challenging for him, so every summer term Mark's wonderful LSA Helen, the one constant in all this change, began to construct the transition book. This detailed where his classroom would be, who his class teacher would be, which teachers would be the same and which teachers would teach him new subjects. Helen would patiently explain the need for the book to each new member of staff, bringing Mark with her and taking a photo of them together to include in the book. In between the information on what was new was sandwiched information on what would remain the same – the reassuring information he so badly needed! He would still be taken to school by Mum, and Mum would still pick him up from the same spot. His lunch would be the same – he would have the same lunchbox and its contents would usually be the same. He would still see the familiar staff in the special needs department. Each year we would try to identify a member of staff he had really connected with and who understood his challenges and talents. With their permission he could find and talk to them at a certain time if he became worried. This person turned out to be, more often than not, his class teacher from the previous year!

Crucially for Mark he knew he would still have his LSA Helen, who helped make every change bearable. Children with autism frequently have more than one LSA in mainstream education to avoid over-dependence on one individual. Usually the new academic year brings a new LSA just at the time when absolutely everything else changes. It takes time for the new LSA to understand each unique child with autism, so there is inevitably a lag in the depth of support just at a time of maximum change. Mark was incredibly fortunate that Helen remained his constant across all these changes and when

Helen was not available he had another familiar and trusted LSA, Sandra, whom he was comfortable with and knew well.

I would advocate a system that involves the known LSA guiding the change across the year group and gradually handing over mid-year to the next LSA, when the routine has become familiar. I know this has already been accomplished in one school and I believe it to be an effective and kind practice. To avoid over-dependence on one individual, the allocation of two LSAs remains a good idea.

Constructing a transition book in the form of a Social Story™ served three important purposes. First, it allowed Mark to become familiar with the unfamiliar, by reading it over and over again. Second, it introduced him to the people who would be teaching him the following year in person, which helped his anxiety and also gave him a concrete photo of them to study over the holidays. Third, it allowed the new teacher to meet 'the child with autism' who he or she would be teaching next term, and this often relieved some anxiety on their part too.

Writing a Social Story about such a difficult topic required language that was not only literal, accurate and positive, but also engaging for Mark to read and listen to. Because he spent a lot of time on his computer games, I used this language to explain that moving up a year at school was similar to going up a level in a computer game. Because going up a level in a game implied that the player had achieved a certain level and was awarded the progression to the next level, this gave a different flavour to going up a year at school, which now appeared more of an achievement and not so much of a wrench. Not all children with autism can understand and therefore benefit from analogy, but for those who do, it can offer a comforting and engaging dimension to a Social Story™. Several parents have told me that using the video game terminology has helped their children too when explaining the need to change years at school.

I am moving up a level to year 3

At school I am Year 2. At the end of the summer term I will have completed Year 2. Next term I will be moving up a level to Year 3.

Completing a level in a video game shows my skills have improved and I am ready to move up to a higher level. Completing Year 2 at school shows my skills have improved and I am ready to move up to Year 3.

There are many things that will be the same in Year 3. A few things will be new. This is okay. This happens when I complete a level and move up to the next one, just like when I play a video game.

Next term I will be in ... class. My teacher will usually be Mrs M. This is a picture of Mrs M and my class door.

The children in my class will mostly be the same. There may be a few new children. Mrs B will still help me in class.

I will still go into school through the front door. I will hang my coat up on a new hook outside my class door, just like in Year 2. The hook will have my name on it. Here is a picture of my new hook.

I will still bring my own lunch box, just like in Year 2, and Mum will usually give me the same lunch in my lunch box. Usually at lunchtime I will still have lunch in the dining room, just like in Year 2.

Mr P will usually teach me Art. Art lessons will be in the Art Room. This is a picture of Mr P. There are more materials and more space to use in the art room.

Mr F or Mr G will teach me Games. This is a picture of Mr F and Mr G. Games lessons will usually be held on the games field.

Assembly will usually still be in the hall. I may still use the toilets beside the library door. I will still have some lessons in the special needs department with Mrs H.

I may still talk to Mrs A. Mrs A is usually in the library at lunch break.

Mrs B will always be happy to help me too.

In Year 3, at the end of the school day I will still usually be met by Mum at the back playground door.

When I move up a level to Year 3 many things will be the same. A few things will be new. This is okay. I will be learning new skills.

Moving up a level means I have completed Year 2 and am ready for the next level in Year 3!

Noise in School

What is a fire drill?

Most institutions have fire drills so that staff and visitors will know what to do in the case of a fire. This is because delay in leaving a building can lead to fatalities as fires spread very rapidly. Stopping what we are doing and following directions on hearing a fire bell allows us to take advantage of any instructions that may keep us safe in the event of a fire, for example which staircases and exits to use. This is all only common sense and most neurotypicals, although irritated by the disruption caused by a fire drill, will be compliant with its requirements.

In schools there is a responsibility on the teacher to collect the class together, which may be a group of up to 30 children or more, and practise leaving the classroom in an orderly fashion so there is no panic and no one gets left behind. Despite never having more than one or two verbal instructions from adults about obeying instructions, most neurotypical children will also usually comply.

The child with autism has three very important disadvantages in this situation. First, as many children with autism are thought to have sensory integration difficulties, the loud and persistent fire bell may be experienced as a very painful stimulus. Of course, its purpose is to alert people and so it is meant to be very loud, and of a frequency and tone that is almost impossible to ignore. However, this painful stimulus may activate the child with autism to a flight or fight response and cause extreme distress. Second, there is a sudden change in activity that requires an immediate response without explanation. Third, there is a large exodus of children into the playground, with lines of children moving close to each other on stairs and in corridors, so in the midst of his physical distress the child has to navigate what feels like social chaos, without social understanding about what is happening and why and when it will end. His levels of bewilderment and anxiety begin to catapult up. What is more, because of his lack of generalisation (due to poor context sensitivity and weak central coherence) a fire drill that takes place in a science lesson may be a completely new experience even though he had a drill in an English lesson a week before.

Mark certainly appeared to find the fire drill extremely uncomfortable, and became distressed when the fire bell rang, holding his hands over his ears. He confirmed to me that the noise 'hurt'. As with many sensory-seated behaviours, the anxiety about the possibility of a fire drill happening at any random time became a background anxiety for him, building each day. For some children this fear can build into a reluctance to attend school. As neurotypicals we would become very anxious too if an extremely painful experience was likely to happen at any time to us without warning or reason in our workplace. We might certainly be reluctant to go to work until it had been sorted out. We would, however, be able to tell people how uncomfortable it was for us, and request that changes were made to make us more comfortable.

To make sense of the context of the fire drill Mark needed social information about the purpose of the fire bell and the teacher's thoughts and intentions behind her instructions. Understanding the logic of repeating an action so that it becomes automatic under duress was also important information for him to know. Being mindful of the fact that the teacher is in charge and knows how to keep the children safe helps neurotypical children comply, and this information also needed to be shared with Mark.

Once written, the Story was read to him each evening for the week before a pre-planned drill and on the morning of the drill he read it through with Helen, his LSA. It markedly improved his compliance, although it was clear he remained uncomfortable with the noise. To reduce his anxiety the school would always give his LSA warning of an upcoming fire drill and so we were able to prepare him by reading the Story. Over time he needed the Story less and less to comply. However, the sensory discomfort remained undiminished as he was unable to use ear defenders or headphones because they might prevent him hearing instructions and could compromise his safety in the event of a real fire.

It was important to help him have social understanding of the situation, and although the noise remained uncomfortable for him, he began to comprehend that it was a safety procedure and that it would stop. This understanding helped him bear the discomfort of the noise.

Each time Mark transitioned into a new stage of education the 'What is a fire drill?' Story was refreshed and updated. Most recently he has been working as an apprentice in an office environment and has been compliant with the fire drill there without having to review the Story. In fact, he did not mention that he had experienced a fire drill at all until I specifically asked him. Astonished and delighted, I asked him how he had managed it. He replied, 'It was okay; the fire bell still hurts, but I know why it has to be so loud.' Mission accomplished.

What is a fire drill?

Sometimes at school a bell rings three times.
After three rings it stops. This bell usually
means that the lesson is finished and it is time
to start the next activity on the timetable.

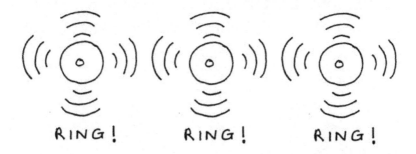

RING!   RING!   RING!

Sometimes a very loud bell will ring at school.
This bell rings for a long time. This bell means it
is a fire drill. The bell for a fire drill is very loud
so everyone hears it.

RING..........!!!!!

A fire drill is pretend. It is a practice so that all the children and adults will know what to do if there is a real fire.

The teacher knows all about fire drills and how to keep children safe. When all the children are quiet everyone can hear the teacher's instructions. Listening to the teacher's instructions is important. This helps keep me safe.

The teacher usually asks everyone to stop their work quickly. Stopping work quickly helps all the children to leave the school building quickly. Leaving quickly is important because fires sometimes spread quickly in buildings. I may finish my work later. This is okay.

Next, the teacher usually asks all the children to line up at the door.

Standing in a line with one child behind another child is called lining up. Moving in a line is a safe and quick way to move lots of children in school.

When everyone has lined up the teacher leads the line of children downstairs into the playground. There is usually an adult at the back of the line to make sure no one has been left behind.

When fire drill is finished the teacher usually tells the class to walk back in line to the classroom.

The teacher will be pleased with me for trying to stop work quickly, being quiet and lining up. The teacher may give me a 'Well done' sticker.

Why do senior school teachers use loud voices?

When Mark was moving from a mixed-sex junior school into an all-boy senior school the junior staff raised a concern that he may find the level of shouting by the mainly male teaching staff uncomfortable. Many children with autism find loud noise, and in particular shouting, extremely uncomfortable or painful due to sensory integration disorder coupled with poor social understanding of the situation.

In his junior school class his quiet spoken class teacher, who understood his needs well, had developed a signal that she would make to Mark to warn him if she needed to raise her voice, and he was then much more able to tolerate the increase level of sound. This worked well.

In the senior school playground, and sometimes during the lessons, staff would raise their voices, or shout, in order to get the students' attention quickly. Although his new form teacher would be aware of the signal his junior teacher had developed with Mark, many others in the senior school would not.

On one of the transition days that Mark went to before entering senior school I observed the environment and noted his reaction to the new surroundings. I was wearing my 'Aspie specs' and was on the lookout for information he might be missing. I noticed that he flinched and covered his ears on several occasions when the teacher raised his voice to gain the attention of another older class. In the playground when this happened again it clearly caused him anxiety. It was obvious a Social Story™ was going to be needed as well as some practical concrete work on understanding loud voices in school before he started the new year.

When Mark was calm and and all was quiet that weekend we sat down together to draw pictures of what the senior school was like. I asked him what senior school sounded like and he said, 'Too loud!' We talked and drew students and teachers and he pointed to the teachers and said again, 'Too loud'. I told him that the teachers *needed* to be loud so that the senior students could hear them because some senior students had deeper, stronger voices than junior students. He looked interested. I thought I had identified the topic and wrote the Story.

The Story and its illustration took many many drafts and nearly a week of work before I felt it adhered to all the criteria and addressed what he needed to know. The illustrations followed the genre Mark was comfortable with, only this time he was not included in the pictures until the last page.

I introduced the idea of needing to use a loud voice by first of all modelling it at home when our family was noisy. I demonstrated to him that sometimes when everyone was sat around the dinner table waiting to be served and talking excitedly in loud voices I needed to ask a question. It was a question everyone would like to hear, 'Who wants chocolate cake?' but no one could hear me when I used a quiet voice. It was only when I raised my voice that everyone heard me and answered my question. I would comment to him, 'No one can hear me. I need a louder voice!' Occasionally I would use a hand signal that showed my increasing volume between my thumb and forefinger like the volume control display on a digital radio interface.

The Story was then introduced and read to him at a quiet, calm time each evening in the week before the next visit to the senior playground. The result was a definite improvement in his ability to cope with the noise. The noise of shouting was still uncomfortable for him, and would still be today; however, understanding why it needed to be loud helped him to tolerate it.

A Social Story™ cannot remove the sensation and the actual discomfort caused by sound, so we were always mindful that a Story like this was never used to make him *endure* noise. Because of his heightened sensitivity to noise, his lovely LSA would take him to a quiet place when there was likely to be sustained loud noise and this helped develop his confidence that school would never become intolerable because of noise. Occasionally he would be allowed the use of earphones too, for example on a school trip, where noise would be condensed within an enclosed space on a bus or a coach. Nowadays many schools are beginning to recognise the impact of sensory integration differences in children with autism and as a result many more children are made more comfortable within their school day with the use of headphones and earphones.

I have sometimes been asked to write Stories around a sudden escape response to a situation at school, and although of course there may be many various triggers, the first one to explore should always be the noise level, followed by the demand level made on the child. For both these difficulties, moving quickly away brings immediate relief to the child. Both parents and professionals need to be aware that our children do not readily ask for help due to their theory of mind differences, but use their own immediate escape response to make themselves more comfortable. A Social Story, along with practical implementation, may help.

Why do senior school teachers use loud voices?

In senior school many students like to play football or another game at break time. Many senior students have deep, strong voices. Sometimes when senior students are playing they make a lot of noise. Sometimes they make a lot of noise when they are in lessons too.

At school there is usually a teacher in charge of the students. It is his job to keep the students safe and to teach them new skills.

Sometimes the teacher wants the students to be quiet quickly so that he can give them a message or an instruction. The students may not hear him if he uses a quiet voice. To make them listen quickly the teacher may make his voice loud. He may shout. This is okay – the teacher needs to use a loud voice.

Senior students make more noise than junior students so the senior teachers often use loud voices to make them listen quickly. This is okay.

I will try to stay calm and listen when the senior teacher shouts. I will work on remembering that the senior teacher needs to use a loud voice. I may think to myself 'It's okay, he needs to use a loud voice.'

Trying to stay calm and listening when the senior teacher shouts is a mature and intelligent thing to do. My form teacher will be pleased with me and may give me a house point.

What volume level is best for headphones?

In order to remain calm and self-regulated in a noisy environment Mark would frequently wear headphones and play music through them. Later on he developed a tolerance for earphones worn inside the ear instead of headphones. Sometimes it was clear to us that the environment was noisy, but at other times I had to refocus from his perspective to understand that although the environment was comfortable for me, it may be uncomfortable for him. During long car journeys, which felt relatively quiet and restful to me, he had a different perception. Unable to fade sounds that were not relevant to him into the background, he needed to cut out some sounds physically and replace them with the comfortable and familiar ones of his choice of music. He recently told me that some sounds were particularly difficult to ignore, such as someone humming out of tune because he was continually alert to the difference in tone and pitch between the music as it should be played by instruments and the hum produced by a human being! Interestingly, he also reported that when he played his music he could see the characters from the music in his mind and that was very relaxing.

However, his brothers sitting next to him in the car complained that the noise leaking from his headphones was irritating and made it difficult for them to relax. When they asked him to turn the volume down he was adamant that only he could hear the music when he had headphones on. So there was a need to share some social information that his theory of mind difference was preventing him from understanding, i.e. the physical perception of noise by others coming from his headphones and how uncomfortable this made others feel. I also needed to explore what levels of volume would allow him to hear his music but at the same time be comfortable for others around him.

I had been using Comic Strip Conversations successfully for some time and Mark was now very familiar with thought and speech bubbles from our drawing conversations. I suggested that it would be helpful and even fun to develop a 'hearing' bubble. We drew some together. He chose a design he liked which was used in the following Story.

First I drew Mark with his hearing bubble containing musical notes to represent what he was hearing. Then I drew another boy close to him and drew him a hearing bubble. I asked Mark what the boy could hear of his music. He replied, 'Nothing, because I have earphones on'. I suggested that the boy might hear noise from the music when it was on a high volume. I guessed that it may annoy the boy because it was a buzzing or thumping, not the real music. I put 'zzzzzthump' in the boy's hearing bubble. I went on to guess that the boy may be thinking 'that noise is annoying' and wrote it in a thought bubble. Mark looked very interested – he is particularly irritated by buzzing and repetitive drumming or thumping noises himself.

I had identified the topic for the Social Story™ which was what others' experience of the music might be. The use of a drawing conversation has nearly always shed light on some very surprising neurotypical perspectives for Mark and some totally unexpected autistic perspectives for me.

The Story was originally written without reference to volume. Then I decided it might help to identify the specific levels at which the headphone volume became a nuisance to others. So we did an experiment. I wore my headphones and raised the volume steadily. Mark noted down when he could hear them and at what volume setting it was. I then did the same for him, so we were able to identify specific levels of volume relevant to his current headphones.

The Story was introduced a week before a long car trip to visit relatives. I noticed Mark checking the volume setting on his headphones before putting them on. His brothers reported a great improvement! The great thing about this Story is that the illustrations were almost complete from the drawing conversation before the Story was written!

Because children with autism may be less able to guess another person's physical experience of a situation, giving them a practical experience of what others perceive is sometimes a critical step, although of course not always possible. The above experiment can also work well when working on voice volume, with one person speaking at different volumes and the child recording a comfort scale. Roles are then reversed. A meaningful signal is developed to represent a reduction in volume and is practised until the volume becomes comfortable for the other person. This is a very useful hand signal to have when out and about!

The volume level numbers in this Story are obviously for one particular set of headphones. Readers wishing to use the format should check the specific volume levels in their child's headphones and adjust them accordingly within the illustrations and texts. As Mark changed headphone sets we had to do this for him too. The Story needs to be accurate.

What volume is best for headphones?

Many people enjoy listening to their favourite music on headphones. I enjoy listening to my favourite music on my headphones. This helps me to relax and keeps me calm. This is an okay thing to do.

My headphones have a volume control from 0 to 10. When someone listens to music with headphones at a volume level 4 or below no one else can hear sound coming from the headphones. The person listening to the music with headphones can enjoy their music and the people nearby can relax.

When someone listens to music with headphones at a volume above level 4 the people near them can hear the music. To the people nearby the music sounds like a loud buzzing or thumping noise. This can make it difficult for the person nearby to relax.

When I have the volume on my headphones above level 4 I may be unable to hear instructions that can alert me to danger and keep me safe. I may need to be able to hear to keep myself and other children safe around me.

When using my headphones I will try to remember to keep the volume at level 4 or below, then I can enjoy my music, relax and stay safe and others around me can relax too.

VOLUME 4 or 3 or 2 or 1

A plan for classroom noise

Our children with autism may have an absolute intolerance of small noises that many neurotypicals do not even notice. These noises, such as a fellow student tapping his pencil on his desk or drumming his fingers or the hum of air conditioning, can be experienced at the same intensity as the teacher's voice in the classroom, making it difficult to concentrate on what he or she is saying. Neurotypicals are able to fade these noises into the background without any thought, it just happens for us automatically, allowing us to pay attention only to the relevant social noise in the situation. We can take no credit for this ability, we have not learned it as a skill, it is simply innate, and this means we can have little concept about what life might be like in this noisy world of ours for those who do not have this ability through no fault of their own.

However, we have all had some experience of conversations taking place in noisy, busy places where concentration on our companion's words is nearly impossible due to the high level of background noise. We can therefore recall the effort of concentrating on picking out our companion's words and how this soon becomes exhausting. Extrapolating this feeling into a constant day in, day out experience gives us some idea of how difficult this must be for our young people.

Sometimes a child may find the noise completely intolerable. Often, because he has a different theory of mind, he is unaware of what others think or know, and therefore instead of asking for help he may try to solve the situation himself, seeking immediate relief and comfort. Unfortunately, his response may be to either leave the situation, regardless of whether it is safe to do so, or to try to forcibly stop the noise.

My aim has always been to help Mark first understand a situation by sharing information with him, and then second, empower him to make himself comfortable in a way that does not make others hostile or uncomfortable. If he can identify situations that are likely to be noisy, this allows him to bring supports to help his comfort. He never goes anywhere without his earphones! Using his earphones between lessons at college was helpful, but using earphones during a lesson was not a solution as he would be unable to hear the tutor. Suggesting a *polite* way of asking someone to stop a noise is a good strategy. Giving an example of words to use is important too, as many people may strongly object to being asked to stop humming, particularly if it said as a demand!

The Story required the understanding and support of the class tutor, who was 'on board' and willing to help, and as a result it was successful. With adaptation it was used for family members at home too, again with success. I still often hear Mark ask his Dad, very politely 'Please stop humming Dad, as it makes it tricky for me to concentrate, thank you!' Outside the particular contexts of the classroom or home situation, however, it is unwise and unsafe to request strangers to stop whistling or humming or tapping, so another Story was written which concentrated on the practical solution of using earphones while out and about, and staying safe.

A plan for classroom noise

Usually college students are quiet during a lesson. Sometimes college students make noises during a lesson. Occasionally a student may tap his fingers or hum or tap his foot against a chair. Some students are able to concentrate when there is noise. Other students need quiet to concentrate.

When another student makes a noise I will try to stay calm. My calming tools may help me stay calm. Many college students think staying calm is mature and intelligent.

When calm I may ask the student politely to stop. I may say something like this in a quiet voice:

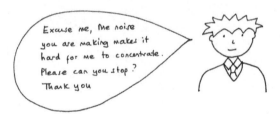

Usually the student will stop. Sometimes the student may continue. If the student continues to make the noise I may ask the tutor for help. The tutor will think that I am a mature and intelligent student.

What is a Social Article?

I initially explained the diagnosis of autism to my son, and other children, using a Social Story™ titled, 'What are worries?' (Timmins, 2016). As Mark grew older he developed more language and became more discerning and there was a need to explain his different perceptions in greater depth. There also was a need to explain why he needed the Social Stories™ or Articles that I was writing for him.

Discussing difficult concepts such as thoughts and feelings with a young person with autism requires the use of concrete visuals along with language that is accessible, familiar and comfortable for them. Using their special interest is a good place to start. It requires the author becoming 'literate' in the special interest. Watching many episodes of Mark's favourite TV, film or Anime series gave me scenarios I could refer to and that illustrated what I wanted to talk about in a way that was interesting, comfortable and meaningful for him. It was also precious time spent together and I learned a lot about not just the special interest, but also why he had chosen it. I am interested in whatever makes him happy as it is an opportunity for me to improve my communication with him and my understanding of him.

Like many young people with autism, Mark has always been interested in IT and computer systems. Tony Attwood describes an adolescent with Asperger syndrome using a computer metaphor to describe the different processing of social information in an autistic brain compared with a neurotypical one (Attwood, 2008). I wanted to explore this further with Mark using a computer analogy within a Social Article. Many children with autism may not be able to understand analogies, so I checked carefully first that Mark had this understanding before beginning.

I explained the way different operating systems in computers required specific file formats in order to open and process files when sharing information. I then explored how in a similar way the transfer of social information needed to be in a specific format when transferring from a neurotypical person to a person with autism. I described each person as having an operating system in their brain, called either a Standard Operating System (SOS) or an Autism Operating System (AOS). Sharing social information in a Social Story™ or Social Article was an effective way of making the information compatible and easy to open and process.

I really wanted to convey the difference between the neurotypical and autism operating systems without loss of self-esteem, giving an idea of equal validity. I also wanted to emphasise that one computer system is not substandard or faulty or broken, but it is processing according to its system and is excellent in its own right. There is no choice involved. This is an important learning point for all those who work with or care about people with autism. I have found that this article also helps neurotypicals to understand the existence of a different processing system and the need for adaptation of information.

So the following Story was written as a Social Article, originally in columns and Times New Roman font, to be respectful of its now more adult audience. Its message can be easily reformatted into a Social Story, with a different font, shorter sentences and more illustrations for a younger or less able audience. I have included the same Story in two different formats here to show the difference format can make to the look of the Story and subsequently to the likely engagement of an individual child.

The comparison to the human brain allowed introduction of the concept of the majority (90%) of neurotypical brains, and the minority of autistic brains (10%) of the population. Further information was needed to explain what numbers the minority might represent in numbers of people so that Mark did not feel further isolated. I used information from Yuko Yoshida's excellent book *How to Be Yourself in a World That's Different*, which demonstrates, in a clear bar chart, that at the time of its publication (2006) the worldwide number of those with autism was approximately the same as the entire population of the UK. Mark therefore belonged to a nation-sized group of people, with their own language, perception and operating system. He was not alone! This idea certainly helped!

What is a Social Article?

A human brain and a computer are similar in many ways. A computer receives information from the outside world through the Internet and other sources like DVD drives and USB flash drives. The computer processes this information and produces output in the form of documents or files.

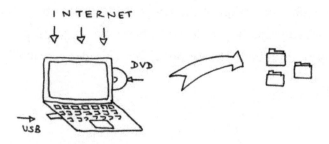

A human brain receives information from the outside world mainly through the senses of sight, hearing, smell, taste, touch and proprioception. The brain processes this information and produces output in the form of language and behaviour.

There are two main kinds of operating systems in computers that process information: Windows (PC computers use this operating system) and MacOSX (Apple computers use this operating system).

To share a file between two computers the format of the file must be compatible with that of the computer it is being sent to, so that it can be opened and processed.

For example, in order for an Apple Mac computer to send a file to a PC computer it must first convert the file from a Pages document into a Word document so that the PC computer can open and process the information.

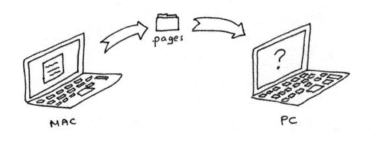

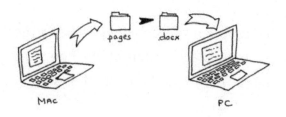

In human brains there are also two main kinds of operating systems. The most common operating system may be called the Standard Operating System or SOS for short. The majority of brains (about 90%) use this system. It is an excellent operating system. The SOS is particularly tuned to social information.

The other operating system may be called the Autism Operating System or AOS for short. The minority of brains (about 10%) use this system. The AOS is also an excellent operating system and in addition may have genius features. Many of the greatest discoveries and inventions by humans come from AOS brains.

When transferring information from an SOS to an AOS, whether it is written information or spoken information, care needs to be taken to send it in a format that can be opened and processed by the other system. This is important because both operating systems have valuable information to share with each other.

A Social Story™ or Article is accurate social information in a specific format that is compatible with the AOS. It is an effective way of transferring social information from an SOS to an AOS. Once opened and read, the information can be shared and used.

Nowadays some computers can run both operating systems and so can process both kinds of information. This is a helpful advance.

In the same way there are many people nowadays who are able to process both kinds of information. Mum is one person who understands both operating systems. This means she knows how to make information compatible with an AOS and write it in a Social Article.

When social information is confusing for an AOS, a Social Story™ or Article may help clarify the information.

What is a Social Article?

A human brain and a computer are similar in many ways. A computer receives information from the outside world through the Internet and other sources like DVD drives and USB flash drives. The computer processes this information and produces output in the form of documents or files.

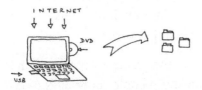

A human brain receives information from the outside world mainly through the senses of sight, hearing, smell, taste, touch and proprioception. The brain processes this information and produces output in the form of language and behaviour.

There are two main kinds of operating systems in computers that process information: Windows (PC computers use this operating system) and MacOSX (Apple computers use this operating system).

To share a file between two computers the format of the file must be compatible with that of the computer it is being sent to, so that it can be opened and processed.

For example, in order for an Apple Mac computer to send a file to a PC computer it must first convert the file from a Pages document into a Word document so that the PC computer can open and process the information.

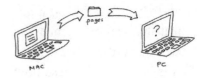

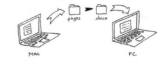

In human brains there are also two main kinds of operating systems. The most common operating system may be called the Standard Operating System or SOS for short. The majority of brains (about 90%) use this system. It is an excellent operating system. The SOS is particularly tuned to social information.

The other operating system may be called the Autism Operating System or AOS for short. The minority of brains (about 10%) use this system. The AOS is also an excellent operating system and in addition may have genius features. Many of the greatest discoveries and inventions by humans come from AOS brains.

When transferring information from an SOS to an AOS, whether it is written information or spoken information, care needs to be taken to send it in a format that can be opened and processed by the other system. This is important because both operating systems have valuable information to share with each other.

A Social Story™ or Article is accurate social information in a specific format that is compatible with the AOS. It is an effective way of transferring social information from an SOS to an AOS. Once opened and read, the information can be shared and used.

Nowadays some computers can run both operating systems and so can process both kinds of information. This is a helpful advance.

In the same way there are many people nowadays who are able to process both kinds of information. Mum is one person who understands both operating systems. This means she knows how to make information compatible with an AOS and write it in a Social Article.

When social information is confusing for an AOS, a Social Story or Article may help clarify the information.

References

Attwood, T. (2008) *The Complete Guide to Asperger Syndrome*. London: Jessica Kingsley Publishers.

Bowler, D.M., Gardiner, J.M. and Grice, S. J. (2000) 'Episodic memory and remembering in adults with Asperger Syndrome.' *Journal of Autism and Developmental Disorders* 30, 4, 295–304.

Brukner, L. (2014) *The Kids' Guide to Staying Awesome and In Control: Simple Stuff to Help Children Regulate their Emotions and Senses*. London: Jessica Kingsley Publishers.

Goddard, L., Dritschel, B., Robinson, S. and Howlin, P. (2014) 'Development of autobiographical memory in children with Autism Spectrum Disorders: deficits, gains, and predictors of performance.' *Development and Psychopathology* 26, 1, 215–228.

Grandin, T. (2006) *Thinking in Pictures*. London: Bloomsbury Publishing.

Gray, C. (1994) *Comic Strip Conversations*. Arlington: Future Horizons.

Gray, C. (2015) *The New Social Story™ Book, 15th Anniversary edition*. Arlington: Future Horizons.

Hodgdon, L. (2013) *Visual Strategies for Improving Communication*. Michigan: QuirkRoberts.

Howley, M. and Arnold, E. (2005) *Revealing the Hidden Social Code*. London: Jessica Kingsley Publishers.

Timmins, S. (2016) *Successful Social Stories™ for Young Children: Growing up with Social Stories™*. London: Jessica Kingsley Publishers.

Vermeulen, P. (2012) *Autism as Context Blindness*. Kansas: AAPC.

Yoshida, Y. (2006) *How to Be Yourself in a World That's Different: An Asperger Syndrome Study Guide for Adolescents*. London: Jessica Kingsley Publishers.

Index

asking for help
  in classroom 72–5
  use of Social Stories™ for 74–5
Arnold, M. 209
Attwood, T. 61, 90, 132, 319–20
award assemblies
  difficulties with 217–19
  use of Comic Strip Conversations
    for 219
  use of Social Stories™ for 219

Bowler, D.M. 44
break time
  difficulties with 164–5
  lining up after 194–6
  supervision of 201–2
  use of Comic Strip Conversations
    for 189
  use of Social Stories™ for 165,
    189, 195, 196, 202
  whistle in 188–9

calmness
  achieving 56–9
  difficulties with 56
  in school 57–8
  and special interests 59, 240–3
  strategies for 56–9
  use of Comic Strip Conversations
    for 242

use of Social Stories™ for 59–61,
  242–3
chasing games 178–9
clarification questions 26–7
classroom noise 315–16
Comic Strip Conversation (CSC)
  award assemblies 219
  break time 189
  calmness 242
  headphones 310
  playground games 170, 183
  and practice 83
  raffles 208
  reading other's intentions 109–10,
    111
  teacher's questions 93
  use of 34–5

empathy through Social Stories™ 41
engagement using Social Stories™
  35–7
episodic memory difficulties 44

fire drills
  difficulties with 296–7
  use of Social Stories™ for 297–8
flexibility through Social Stories™
  40–1
friendships in schools 25–6

teachers
  asking questions 93
  break time supervision 201–2
  and homework 133
  knowledge of 93
  listening to 52–3
  shouting 303–5
  use of Social Articles for 53
  use of Social Stories™ for 94-5,
    304–5
theory of mind
  description of 25
  and friendships 25–6
  and teachers 93–5

Timmins, S. 319
transitions through school
  difficulties with 286–7
  use of Social Stories™ for 288–9
turn-taking 26

Vermeulen, P. 22

worthy opponents 230–1